C000156661

PRAISE FOR

FINANCIAL CRIME
Book of Mentors

"This is the 'Hitchhiker's Guide to the Galaxy' for Financial Crime Fighters - jam-packed full of advice, anecdotes and assistance from industry leaders that have already journeyed far and wide and are sharing candid tales and truths for those that care to follow. A compelling read, and companion for all of us - whether just starting out, as your career progresses or even for those that think they have made it! "

> - **John Cusack**, Chair of the Global Coalition to Fight Financial Crime

"Financial Crime Fighter Book of Mentors is an outstanding resource for financial crime fighters of all levels of experience to learn from the best in the world. I've been lucky enough to work with several of the mentors and I still learned things from them in this book that I didn't know before. This is the type of book that you'll learn from today, but that you can also come back to later on your financial crime fighting journey and take away different lessons. I highly recommend it!"

> - **Craig Timm**, Managing Director, Global Financial Crimes, Bank of America

"Sensational idea for a book: getting the financial crime brains trust together to spill their collective beans on their personal journeys in fighting financial crime is a must-read for anyone interested in this field".

> - **Anthony Quinn**, Founder Arctic Intelligence

"Fantastic personal insights from some of our industry's finest and the closest thing you will find to a handbook on how to be a successful Financial Crime Fighter."

> - **Steve Barnett**, Co-Founder of Gracechurch Financial Crime Prevention

"This book is full of wisdom and career advice not only for those wanting to build a career in fighting financial crime. It also directly speaks to those who need general guidance in career development and how to navigate a career change. The book emphasizes the importance and criticality of coaching and mentoring in developing and retaining great talents as shared by the successful professionals who contributed their personal stories in this book which I really enjoyed reading. An excellent book on financial crime, human development and career management!"

— **Vicky Lee-Salas**, Partner, Financial Services Leader, SGV&Co

"This book is a great "go to" resource for people who are contemplating becoming a financial crime professional, just starting in the profession or a seasoned professional who is working through a complex scenario or trying to make a difficult decision. I've been very lucky throughout my career as I've had access to a number of senior financial crime experts who have always been gracious with their time to offer advice whenever I'm facing a difficult situation/decision, but not everyone might have the same access. The questions answered by the mentors in this book are ones all financial crime professionals face on a regular basis and the advice provided will help the reader work through their financial crime problem in a practical manner or to just remind them of "why" they love this profession, it definitely did for me! I'll be keeping a copy nearby for easy access!"

— **Claudia Hui**, Head of Institutional Bank Financial Crime Risk, Australia and New Zealand and Global Head of Institutional Banking Transaction Monitoring at Macquarie Bank

"A must read for financial crime fighters and managers! Lifted my spirits. Just when you think you are alone in this fight against crime, the stories will resonate with you. Words of wisdom from influential leaders on pitfalls to avoid. More importantly, this book inspires you to take action and challenge yourself to learn continuously."

— **Audrey Sim**, Global Financial Crime Compliance Director at Bank of America

"I have often read online that the most effective life lessons are learned through experience, and what better than to learn from the experience of folks who have seen it and done it all.

The Book of Mentors is a collection of thoughts and experiences of industry veterans in the financial crimes world. The author of the book – Jun Claravall – has interviewed more than thirty of the best in the business to uncover how they broke through and launched their careers. Jun has discovered the one thing all of them have in common: they love what they do in contributing to the fight against financial crimes.

The book allows the reader to go behind the thought process of industry leaders in financial crimes and learn from their experiences on the mindset needed to succeed in the ever-evolving fight against financial crimes. There are many clear-cut and actionable takeaways for forward-thinking financial crimes practitioners.

The industry leaders, many of whom I have had the privilege of working with, collaborating, or just hearing from use examples from their own experience to reveal some of the most interesting stories of how they contributed to real life cases in fighting financial crimes. A couple of stories linking to human trafficking and personal safety of the contributor's family literally gave me goose bumps. A must read for all those in the financial crimes industry!"

- **Shabbir Syed**, Director and Head of APAC Financial Crimes Strategy and Governance with a Leading Global Financial Institution

"Book of Mentors is a must read for all existing and aspiring Financial Crimes experts. This comprehensive book has a wealth of experiences combined with practical advice from a group of 30 Financial Crime Fighters, who have shared the most amazing true stories. This book will act as a guiding light for all challenges that any Financial Crime professionals face. Author has done a wonderful job in putting together all the key and essential ingredients for a successful Financial Crime expert in one book. It was also great to hear that all profits from book sales are donated to fight modern slavery."

- **Sudhakar Aduri**, APAC Sanctions and Anti-Bribery and Corruption Head

FINANCIAL CRIME FIGHTER

Book of Mentors

Practical Career Advice from Leaders in our Profession

Tadeo (Jun) Claravall

Financial Crime Fighter Book of Mentors

Copyright © 2021 by Tadeo (Jun) Claravall
First published 2021
Published by The Financial Crimes
Haymarket NSW Australia 2000
Email: book@thefinancialcrimes.com
URL: http://www.thefinancialcrimes.com

ISBN: 9798474911335 (Paperback)

PUBLISHER'S LEGAL DISCLAIMER

The material in this book is for informational purposes only. As each individual situation is unique, you should use proper discretion before trying any of the information in this book.

This book presents a wide range of opinions about a variety of topics related to financial crime risk, programs, prevention, and careers in anti-financial crime. These opinions reflect the ideas of the author and contributors and are not intended as a substitute for professional and legal advice.

The author and the publisher disclaim responsibility for any adverse effects that may result from the use or application of the information contained in this book.

DEDICATION

I dedicate this book to my loving wife Lanie, my biggest supporter who encouraged me through it all.

To my children Jessica, Paolo, Kayla, and Nicole, I hope this book inspires you to strive to be the absolute best version of yourselves.

To my parents, Tady and Nora Claravall, thank you for instilling in me the value of reading and surrounding me with books growing up.

Thank you, and I love you all more than words can express.

financial crime fighter

[fi-nan-sh*uh*l krahym-fahy-ter]

noun

> 1. any person who prevents, detects, reports, investigates or prosecutes financial crime

mentor

[men-tawr]

noun

> 1. a wise and trusted counsellor or teacher
> 2. an influential senior sponsor or supporter

CONTENTS

FINANCIAL CRIME FIGHTER
Book of Mentors

WHY I WROTE THIS BOOK

To explain why I wrote this book, I need to start with when.

I left my role as Managing Director and Asia Pacific Executive for Global Financial Crimes Compliance at Bank of America in May 2019 closing out almost 26 years of working in the industry, which interestingly also started at Bank of America in June 1993 when I was fresh out of university.

The intervening years led me to stints at JPMorgan Chase, UBS AG, and Citibank across four countries in the Asia Pacific, where I had the privilege to work with and for some remarkable people, built a career in anti-financial crime and honed my leadership and mentoring skills.

As often happens at forks in the path, semi-retirement brought forward important life questions. In my case, I pondered about my contribution to society and two questions in particular. First, is there something I could do at scale to help my fellow financial crime fighters deal with the daily challenges of their work? Second, as for broader society I thought about what I can do to help its most vulnerable members.

The idea of writing a book with all profits going to charity came to me over a few weeks of exploring these questions and aligning the answer to something I love doing, which is mentoring.

So, one morning I started writing down some of the lessons I learned and applied in my life and career based on the questions I frequently get asked by mentees and questions I've asked my mentors throughout my career. My goal was to create a kind of 'guidebook' offering career advice for financial crime fighters.

Then it hit me. Wouldn't the book be more impactful if I invited global leaders in anti-financial crime to participate so instead of just one mentor, my fellow financial crime fighters could have a group of mentors to learn from?

The result is the book that you are holding in your hands. Close to 300 pages of timeless wisdom from 30 senior leaders in our profession answering 18 questions mentees frequently ask mentors in our field of anti-financial crime.

Personally, this is a book that I would like to read and something that I wish I had with me during my career. No matter what work situation or problem you may be facing presently, there is a good chance that some information, insight, or lesson in this book that might be of help. Therefore, it is deeply satisfying to think that this book has the potential of changing someone's life and career.

HOW TO READ THIS BOOK

Before beginning the book, you will profit greatly if you recognize the fact that this book was not written to entertain. You don't even need to read this book in any order or sequence. Rather, whatever your biggest issue, problem or concern is now, you should go to the section of this book that might be able to help give you answers and insights on how some of the best in the world at what we do have handled the same problem in the past and how that worked out for them. It's like having a personal board of directors showing you the path to success and the pitfalls to avoid.

When reading this book, imagine you're meeting with these mentors, and they are giving you a daily, personal challenge and advice on how to become the best financial crime fighter you can be.

A favourite author of mine Jim Rohn once wrote, "you are the average of the five people you spend the most time with". I found this to be true in my career. My advice is for you to surround yourself with other successful leaders, and this book is one convenient and effective way of doing that.

My hope is that you'll find five or more leaders and mentors here that you will resonate with. But don't just read their words. Study it and act on their advice. Try some of it out. If it fits, keep doing it. If it doesn't, set it aside and try someone else's advice. That's my formula for success. Simple but not easy. Then again nothing worthwhile is easy.

THE MENTORS

Any greatness in this book comes from the people who contributed.

Here are 30 from the world's best who have generously shared advice, stories and lessons that form the essence of this book.

1. John CUSACK, Chair of the Global Coalition to Fight Financial Crime
2. Anthony NAPPI, Former Citibank Global Head of Operational Risk and Control for the Consumer Bank
3. Jaikumar (Jai) RAMASWAMY, Chief Risk & Compliance Officer at cLabs
4. William Scott GROB, Association of Certified Anti-Money Laundering Specialists (ACAMS) AML Director for the Americas
5. Patricia SULLIVAN, Global Head of Financial Crime Business Control & Oversight, Deutsche Bank; Executive Board Member Lawyers Without Borders
6. Matt FRIEDMAN, Modern Slavery Expert and CEO of The Mekong Club
7. Rod FRANCIS, Senior Managing Director and Asia Lead for the Financial Crime Compliance Practice at FTI Consulting
8. Jason HOLT, Interim Group Head of GFCC at a Global Asset Manager
9. Guillermo HORTA, Global Head and Chief Anti-Money Laundering Officer at Scotiabank International Bank
10. Paul (Paddy) O'HARA, Former Head of FCC at Standard Chartered Bank
11. Stevenson MUNRO, Global Head, Economic Sanctions Compliance, High-Risk Clients and Emerging Threats at Standard Chartered Bank
12. Mel Georgie B. RACELA, Executive Director, Anti-Money Laundering Council (Philippines)
13. Will BROWN, Head of Corporate Governance Recruitment at Hamlyn Williams

14. Carlos GARCIA PAVIA, Global Head of Screening, Surveillance, and Regulatory Conduct Analytics at HSBC
15. Scott BURTON, Asia Pacific Head of Anti-Financial Crime at Deutsche Bank
16. Lucy MASTERS, Head of Audit Covering Financial Crime, Compliance and Conduct and Specialist Businesses at Westpac
17. Maggie QIU, Head of Sanctions for Greater China and North Asia at Standard Chartered Bank
18. John FOGARTY, Executive General Manager Financial Crime Compliance, and MLRO at the Commonwealth Bank of Australia
19. Martin James WALLIS, Chief Operating Officer at FINTRAIL
20. Jessica HODSON, Senior Head-hunter Partner at Investigo
21. Armina ANTONIOU, General Manager Financial Crime Risk at Tabcorp (Australia)
22. Marlene MELI, Financial Crime Mitigation Expert
23. Nicholas TURNER, Of Counsel in the Hong Kong Office of Steptoe and Johnson
24. Marta Lia REQUEIJO, Head of Financial Crime Compliance and MLRO for ClearBank UK
25. Anthony QUINN, Founder at Arctic Intelligence
26. Eric FAVILA, Senior Principal at Promontory Financial Group, an IBM Company
27. Deborah YOUNG, Founding CEO of the RegTech Association
28. Yvette CHEAK, Seasoned Banking Compliance Professional in Singapore
29. Abtar RANDHAWA, Global Financial Crime Audit Executive
30. Jerome MICHAILIDIS, Head of Norms and Procedures at BNP Paribas

You must appreciate that all these people are busy beyond belief, and I expected I would get short, rushed responses at best. But to my surprise majority of them gave some of the most thoughtful and insightful answers I'd ever expect. For that, I'm incredibly grateful.

It was a joy and a privilege to collaborate with the 30 senior leaders in this book.

THE QUESTIONS

Below are the 18 questions I asked the 30 senior leaders to answer. My request was for them to answer at least 5. Most answered eight questions or more, and a few answered all 18.

Think of this book as a portal into the minds of some of the most knowledgeable mentors in financial crime-fighting today, answering some important questions, the answers to which may help you become a more effective financial crime fighter and become even more successful in your career.

1. How did you start your Financial Crime Fighting career? What inspired you to take this course in life?
2. In your eyes, what is the most difficult part of your job as a financial crime fighter? How do you handle it?
3. Do you have a unique or interesting financial crime-fighting story that you can share?
4. What do you think is the most effective strategy to fighting financial crime?
5. Do you believe there is more that we can do to fight financial crime? If so, what more?
6. What would you change about financial crime risk and compliance programs?
7. What is the role of technology in your current job? Do you think it will be more critical with the threat of COVID-19?
8. If financial crime fighters want to stay relevant in this coming age of A.I. and machine learning technologies, what do you think are the most important steps for them to take?
9. Knowing what you now know, what are some mistakes you've made that you want other financial crime fighters to learn from or avoid?
10. Is there any one mistake you find financial crime fighters making over and over in their careers?
11. What failures have you learned from the most that have contributed to your career success?

12. When you hear the term 'career success', what/who comes to mind? What are your top 3 tips for career success?
13. Was there ever a time when you wished you took a different career path? Why did you decide to stay in/ return to financial crime?
14. How do you feel about mentoring? Do you believe that it can help in developing a financial crime fighter's career? Are there any mentoring stories that you can share?
15. What is your typical daily schedule? Do you have any hints for managing work-related stress? How do you stay productive?
16. It can be challenging to find time for yourself in any career. Do you have any helpful tips on how to do this successfully?
17. If you could give advice to your younger self just entering our profession, what would it be?
18. If you had a chance to get a message out to all Financial Crime Fighters in the world, what would you write?

THE CHARITY

All profits from the sale of this book will forever be donated to support efforts to fight modern slavery.

Modern slavery generates USD150 billion in criminal proceeds every year. There are over 40 million people trapped in modern slavery world-wide, with only 0.2% helped each year. One in four are children, and almost three quarters (71%) are women and girls.

The first charity to benefit is The Mekong Club (https://themekong-club.org/).

The Mekong Club helps fight against modern slavery by mobilizing businesses to bring about sustainable practices towards the fight against modern slavery.

The Mekong Club has years of experience working with companies and their many dedicated employees, providing practical tools, strategic thinking, and a forum to join together and stop slavery in our lifetime.

By purchasing this book, you are helping rid the world of this serious problem affecting some of the most vulnerable people in society.

MY CHALLENGE TO YOU

"Life's lessons only begin with books. They don't stop there"
                                                    - Rusticus

Don't just be inspired, be inspirational.

You may get inspired by the mentors your will meet in this book and motivated by their stories. But don't just admire them. Use their hard-earned lessons. Improve on them. Make them your own. Then become an inspiration to others.

One of my favourite discoveries in producing this book was that nearly all the contributing senior leaders made mistakes and had failure experiences that appear to have left a deep impression on them and, as a result, equipped them with unique insight and knowledge that helped transform them into the leaders that they are today. Through the pages of this book, you can now learn easily what these leaders learned with great difficulty. I think that alone makes your investment of time and money on this book more than worth it.

But I will only consider this book a success if it incites you to action and take your career into your own hands and make you realize that what others have done, you can do the same.

I hope that one day we would meet, and you will tell me how you used some of the information in this book and how it worked out for you.

Thank you and continue fighting the good fight!

Tadeo (Jun) Claravall
Sydney, Australia - October 2021

FINANCIAL CRIME FIGHTER

Book of Mentors

Practical Career Advice from Leaders in our Profession

Tadeo (Jun) Claravall

FIRST, A THANK YOU TO OUR MENTORS:

Thank you, John Cusack, Marta Lia Requeijo, Nicholas (Nick) Turner, Mel Georgie B. Racela, Anthony Nappi, Jerome Michailidis, Lucy Masters, Jason Holt, Rod Francis, Scott Burton, Armina Antoniou, Carlos Garcia Pavia, Paul (Paddy) O'Hara, Will Brown, Dr William Scott Grob, Jessica Hodson, Guillermo (Memo) Horta, Marlene Meli, Stevenson (Steve) Munro, Maggie Qiu, Jaikumar (Jai) Ramaswamy, Patricia (Trish) Sullivan, Martin James Wallis, John Fogarty, Matt Friedman, Yvette Cheak, Eric Favila, Anthony Quinn, Abtar Randhawa, and Deborah Young

Your stories, advice and lessons are the essence of this book. Thank you for your time and generosity in sharing your brilliant insights and for some, painful lessons learned.

May the good you share with the world be returned to you thousand-fold.

How did you
start your Financial
Crime Fighting
career?
What inspired you to take
this course in life?

QUESTION 1

TADEO (JUN) CLARAVALL: "From the time I was young, I thought of myself as a practical idealist, although, of course, I did not know that term as a child. So, getting into a profession like the anti-financial crime that involves doing good and fighting evil as the mission felt like home to me.

It all started in 1999. I was an accountant for Chase Manhattan Bank, Manila Branch when I came across a draft copy of the U.S.A. PATRIOT Act. It was fascinating for me to read about an area of regulatory compliance whose objective was to fight financial crime. At the tender age of 26, I decided that should there be an opportunity for me within the bank to work in this area, that I would explore it.

When the tragic events of September 11, 2001 occurred and terrorism financing became an essential focus for regulators, global banks started beefing up their Anti-Money Laundering and Counter-Terrorism Financing (AML/ CTF) teams. I was working at the now merged JPMorgan Chase Bank in Manila, have moved out of finance into compliance. As with most in the industry, the bank started building its AML/ CTF teams under the Compliance umbrella.

At JPMorgan in the Asia Pacific, of which the Manila Branch was part of, the person leading the charge for AML/ CTF was a former H.K. Police Detective, Peter Hazlewood, a bright, charming, and driven financial crime professional who I believe was one of the pioneers for AML/ CTF Compliance in the Asia Pacific region. He not only acted the part, but he looked the part as well since he looked like he could pass for a James Bond 007 character (one of the good guys).

As luck would have it, in May 2002, he flew to Manila from Singapore, where he is based, to investigate an internal fraud event. He asked if I could assist him, which I gladly did. That did it for me. I was hooked. My curiosity about financial crime became a passion, and I told Peter that should he ever need someone for his team that I would want to be considered.

Question 1: "How did you start your Financial Crime Fighting career? What inspired you to take this course in life?"

3

One morning in September 2002, Peter left me a voice mail saying that he's gotten approval for my family and me to move to Singapore if I'm still interested in working for him. I could not contain my excitement. I called my wife and let her listen to the voice mail herself and asked her what she thought.

We were on a plane to Singapore in January 2003 to start my new career as a financial crime fighter. That started my now close to a 20-year career in fighting financial crime."

ANTHONY QUINN: "Back in 2006, I was a Project Manager working in the banking sector when AML laws were first being introduced and the challenge and opportunity to do something, meaningful and positive resonated with me and, I jumped at the opportunity when Macquarie Bank head-hunted me from Westpac to establish and run the Anti-Money Laundering and Counter-Terrorism Financing Program for the retail arm of the bank.

I was responsible for leading a multi-disciplinary project team and delivering capabilities ranging from governance, customer due diligence, employment screening, training, transaction monitoring, regulatory reporting, and much more before handing various systems, procedures, and controls to various operating groups to manage and maintain in a business-as-usual capacity.

After successfully delivering this, the first major bank in the Australian market to do so, I was recruited again to run the FATCA program for the same division of Macquarie so, was there as a contractor for nearly 9 years before setting up Arctic Intelligence."

NICK TURNER: "I was fortunate to join Citi as a Compliance Management Associate in New York right out of law school. For two years, I rotated around the bank to learn different areas of compliance.

My first rotation was in trade finance, where I learned about economic sanctions and trade-based money laundering. Then, I spent a year on an anti-money laundering remediation project in California. After that, I was hooked."

JOHN CUSACK: "Probably being in the right place at the right time and running towards trouble as I saw it, first finding and investigating illicit funds from former Nigerian President Sani Abacha and a little later taking the lead to formulate a comprehensive response following the 9/11 Attacks on America.

I was a lawyer that transited into compliance who transited into fighting financial crime. By the time the need arose, I had established myself within a large international financial institution with a high inherent risk profile for financial crime and was also serious about tackling it. However, running towards trouble isn't wise unless you can count on support and reinforcements, which I was able to muster and depend on."

YVETTE CHEAK: "I started as soon as Singapore introduced Regulations on control of Money Laundering and when I was Chair of the ABS Standing Committee on Compliance and Self Governance in the 1980s."

JOHN FOGARTY: "I started my career in the NSW Police Force at the age of 19. I grew up in a large family with six other siblings, all with a strong moral compass. My parents instilled in us a sense of doing what is right, so naturally, when I observed others not doing the right thing, I felt compelled to do something. This sense of purpose followed me through my career to where I now find myself helping the Bank its customers and the broader community."

ROD FRANCIS: "After choosing Banking as my career, I spent the first five years in a client-facing role at RBS in London. I was introduced to Risk and Compliance post an Internal Audit of the unit I had oversight for, and I was invited to join what was then, Compliance and Internal Audit.

My mentor encouraged me to take the opportunity, and I soon realized the criticality of risk and control. This was in the early '90s and by the mid 90's the topic of Anti-Money laundering was fast becoming central to Compliance programs in Financial Institutions. I found the topic fascinating, and I was fortunate and privileged to be involved in UK efforts from the start via the JMLSG. It felt, and it still feels, we are doing something good for society in an industry which often is portrayed in the opposite light."

SCOTT BURTON: "It was more by chance rather than by design. My first introduction to financial crime compliance was a project role, which was focused on bank account opening processes and the mandatory regulatory requirements.

Question 1: "How did you start your Financial Crime Fighting career? What inspired you to take this course in life?"

5

This was a fascinating opportunity at the time and allowed me to understand the fundamentals of banking with knowing your customers, due diligence on customers whilst utilizing a project management approach on regulatory requirements, and implementing these into banking procedures and policies, all of which are still as important today."

MAGGIE QIU: "I started my FCC career with BAML in its FIU unit in the middle of 2008's financial crisis. At that time, I was doing a risk management role with Wachovia, and because it has been bought by Wells Fargo due to a financial crisis, many of my projects are on hold; hence I accepted a headhunter's invitation for an interview with BoA for an AML risk manager role.

Back then, I had little knowledge of AML compliance, and it was the headhunter who inspired me to look beyond the technical knowledge and focus more on those transferable skillsets that can enable me to do well in my next role.

The people I met throughout the interview process also inspired me to join the team. They are all passionate about fighting financial crimes - eager to apply technology know-how and data analysis to detect suspicious transactions and identify AML red flags and patterns. They made me believe the noble cause behind my day job, and I gained the confidence that my previous data-analytical skills combined with good people skills can really add value to the organization."

MARTIN JAMES WALLIS: "I was coming to the end of my career in the British Army, where I had worked throughout in intelligence. Generally, I spent a considerable amount of time understanding and identifying who the bad actors were, what they were doing, and ways to prevent and disrupt their efforts. I found some of the same elements and purpose in fighting financial crime as I learned more. However, it quickly became clear through the scale of the problem that there was still plenty of meaningful work to be done.

I began to speak with some of whom I thought were key leaders in the space, and their passion to combat financial crime was infectious, and I thought this was where I could continue to make an impact.

I was very grateful for the time they afforded me, and this open attitude clearly helped shape my opinion of the sector. The co-founders at FIN-TRAIL both had a deep passion for changing the landscape of financial crime prevention and had created a company that was trying to make a difference and challenge some of the norms within the industry. This resonated with me, and I grasped the opportunity to help play my part."

STEVENSON MUNRO: "It's as simple as paying attention to what I found interesting, and if I have one piece of career advice, it's that. I wouldn't have known any of this at the time. Still, by simply focusing on things that interested me, I created a wholly satisfying career with a central theme around the intersection of economics, law, politics, foreign policy and fighting financial crime.

In my case, as an undergraduate, I studied economics because I found the underlying political debates about macro-economic theory intellectually engaging. It was the political debate about "trickle-down economics," the tax policies, the implication of growing budget deficits, and the domestic and foreign policy of the Regan Administration that caused me to study macro-economic theory as a student. One of the most compelling issues of the time was the economic boycott of South Africa. I can still recall the discussions. The moral imperative was clear; the question we debated was whether economic decisions by individuals and institutions 5000 miles away could create change, or was it solely symbolic?

After graduation, I became a soldier. As a military intelligence officer stationed in a remote, rural area along the East-West German border at the end of the Cold War, I witnessed the truly fascinating events during the last few weeks of 1989 as 40 years of military, economic, and foreign policy exploded. My viewpoint was at a very local level, watching how individuals reacted in the small towns of central Germany as their villages that had been separated by minefields, barbed wire, and watchtowers were suddenly, literally over the span of a weekend, reunited. At the core was the question of the power of economics in this transformation.

Upon reflection, the Army, and military intelligence in particular, not only feed my interest in the intersection of foreign policy and economics, but it taught me the fundamental skills of effective financial crime compliance. The military and financial crime compliance are both essentially about risk assessments and implementing effective deterrent, preventative and detective controls. Both require understanding and prioritizing the threats, figuring out how to prevent and detect if that threat occurring, investigating the indications you've detected, and implementing defined processes and action plans to mitigate that threat as and where you've

Question 1: "How did you start your Financial Crime Fighting career? What inspired you to take this course in life?"

7

found it – and then feeding that knowledge back into your threat assessments and detective and preventative controls.

After law school and while practising law, these intellectual areas of interest led me to learn about and ultimately get hired by the U.S. Treasury Department and its Office of Foreign Assets Control. At the time, it was a largely unknown office in the U.S. government, and the legal practice of economic sanctions was best described as "arcane and nuanced." I found it fascinating. The intersection of sanctions with money laundering and enforcement naturally evolved into the discipline of financial crime compliance, and it's around this intersection that I've defined my career. The only part that was deliberate was to engage in topics that I found fascinating."

MATT FRIEDMAN: "In 2010, I was working with the United Nations. At that time, we determined that out of the estimated 21 million people in modern slavery, only 0.2 percent were being helped globally. When we looked at the numbers, we came to realize that 75 percent of the cases were forced labor, of which 60 percent were associated with supply chains. These figures helped us to understand the relevance of the private sector within this issue.

Armed with this information, I started to travel to Hong Kong to meet with the banking community. With the US$150 billion in profits generated by these crimes annually, many of the banks understood the importance of the problem. But at that time, they didn't have a strategy to move the process forward. Recognizing the important role they could play to be part of the solution, I left the United Nations and set up the Mekong Club. Our goal is to work with the private sector in a positive, supportive manner to help educate and equip companies to address the problem. This was the beginning of my financial crime-fighting career."

MARLENE MELI: "In 2006, when I joined the project team to implement a global compliance screening infrastructure at UBS, I had only limited knowledge about financial crime, money laundering or financing of terrorism. But soon, it became apparent to me how important a sound framework and a powerful infrastructure are.

I was fascinated by the challenge to detect and stop financial crime without compromising customer service and increase operational efficiency, all at the same time. What was, and still is, most important for me to fight financial crime is the fact that behind every dollar laundered, there is a victim – a victim of drug trafficking and drug abuse, human trafficking, and slavery, of tax evasion and lack of access to education."

MARTA LIA REQUEIJO: "Most of my career changes happened through just being open to new opportunities. I did not plan a career in financial crime; I just decided to step outside of my comfort zone and try something new. Because I had so many opportunities to learn and further progress, I was surrounded by mentors that supported me, and I was having so much fun; it has never since occurred to me that I could do something else.

I was attending a Capital Markets Postgraduate Diploma, and some of the papers I submitted focused on upcoming regulatory developments. One of the course tutors worked at the Portuguese Securities Markets Commission - the capital markets regulator - which at the time was hiring. I applied and joined the Supervision Division, where economists – my academic background - and lawyers worked together to assess new regulations and performed on-site visits to supervised entities. This was my first contact with compliance and money laundering regulatory requirements.

When I was later invited to join a global bank to build their money laundering and compliance department, I immediately accepted. This was a particularly challenging role, but my previous experience working at a bank branch and as a regulator was key to overcoming the challenges.

From then on, my career progressed very naturally. New opportunities enabled me to broaden my knowledge and experience not only in the financial crime space but also in building and managing high-performing teams."

JEROME MICHAILIDIS: "Honestly, I 'fell into it' by chance. I had moved to NYC (from central Illinois) and was looking for temp jobs. The agency with which I was working had several Compliance placements, so I had to get myself organized or whatever they had!"

PATRICIA SULLIVAN: "I have long roots in crime-fighting with my father spending his career in the New York City Police Department and many family members also 'on the job.' I attended law school with the objective of becoming a criminal prosecutor and landed my dream job in the Manhattan District Attorney's Office.

Question 1: "How did you start your Financial Crime Fighting career? What inspired you to take this course in life?"

9

I started prosecuting misdemeanors, graduated to felonies, including sex crimes, and spent my final two years in the Frauds Bureau, where my passion for going after white-collar criminals took hold. I took my first job in a bank (UBS) in 2006 in the Regulatory Compliance team, but within a year, an opening came up in the Financial Crime Compliance (FCC) team, and I knew this was the mission for me. I was hesitant to apply for the role as my only prior related experience was as a prosecutor, and I had not been in the bank very long. Still, very supportive colleagues inspired and supported me to go for it. I got the job and never looked back. That was 2007."

ARMINA ANTONIOU: "While in high school, one of the career options I considered was in Law Enforcement. I have always been one to appreciate playing by the rules – I used to play a lot of sports and worked as a referee/umpire, so I had a very healthy respect for rule-following and ensuring that all players were playing fairly. This was definitely why I looked into a career in the police force.

However, heeding my Tiger Mother's words about the financial reward for intellect, looking in the mirror and realizing that I was not as physically gifted as the typical criminals I would want to be apprehending (and not to mention the exploits of Jimmy Smits in LA Law), I decided to study Law at University.

Moving onto life as a lawyer in a big law firm, I always gravitated to the cases where questions of public interest arose, so I enjoyed working on matters that involved trials before regulatory bodies, anti-corruption commissions, and the coroner's court. Probably unusually for a corporate litigator, the aspect of those cases I was most interested in was speaking to the people involved and understanding their stories and their different points of view about the circumstances the court was looking into.

While working as a lawyer, I was sent out on secondment to a big domestic bank to assist in preparing for a regulatory review before AUS-TRAC. The secondment was due to last for "a maximum of 6 weeks." Still, I ended up staying for six months and really enjoyed learning about how corporate entities can contribute to identifying, mitigating, and managing financial crime. It was here I started thinking that there might be other ways that I could put my legal training to use and considered a career in Anti-Financial Crime.

It wasn't until about five years later, when I was working at Tabcorp, that I took up a role as the GM of Financial Crime Risk, and I have loved it ever since."

JASON HOLT: "I think many of us are financial crime fighters of sorts from an early age.

As such, it is not easy to date precisely when my financial crime-fighting career commenced. Although, it was certainly prior to joining law enforcement or banking. My career of sorts is almost certainly marked by one of the following three events.

At about 18 years of age, I worked as an assistant buyer at a large technology firm. Shortly after taking up the role, I looked through the documentation for previous purchases made and found an order for a computer purchased. Still, I could not find the associated purchase order form required to authorize the purchase. On further investigation, I found that the delivery address for the computer was the home address of the previous head buyer (now an ex-employee). This was reported to the Police, who visited the ex-employee at his home, and while they were knocking at the front door, he was busy throwing the computer over his neighbor's fence!

Lessons learned:

- Not all criminals are geniuses, and
- Try and get one step ahead of them; always think about how a criminal might seek to hide their ill-gotten gains.

The second occasion was while walking home after an evening out with friends. I saw a person trying to smash the window of an off-license to steal the alcohol inside. I challenged him and, after a short chase, wrestled him to the ground. While waiting for the Police to arrive, he looked up at me, smiled, and promptly bit me hard in the groin! To sweeten the pain, the Police subsequently contacted me to say the off-licenses management was very grateful for my efforts and wanted to reward me. I should go into the off-license and collect it at some point. Embarrassed to do so, I put this off for a few weeks, but one day passed by the shop and thought I would pop in to introduce myself. On doing so, I was told I couldn't be the person involved as they had already been in to collect their reward. Needless to say, it turned out this was the person who I had detained!

More lessons learned:

Question 1: "How did you start your Financial Crime Fighting career? What inspired you to take this course in life?"

11

- The fight against financial crime can be painful
- Never let your guard down, especially when a criminal is smiling at you
- Don't be slow to accept recognition for your efforts, as others will be happy to step in and take the credit
- Criminals have few, if any, morals and will take advantage of any situation if they can.

In my mid 20's, while working as a financial advisor. Like many such roles at the time, we were measured by how much business we wrote. It seems quite common in such roles to have a rather brash and arrogant colleague, and this was no exception. In fact, Clive was also by far the most successful member of the team. Given his success, management supported him and was perhaps more tolerant of some of his behaviors. We all wondered how it was that he was so much more successful than the rest of us. I, for one, wanted to know the secret of his success so that I could emulate it. He was tight-lipped. Soon enough, we found out what this secret was. It turned out he was getting people to sign up for products that had no intention of paying for them; in the meantime, he collected the commission, and no doubt shared some of this with the 3rd parties. Of course, after he was found out, they fired him. It appeared to me that criminals were everywhere, and this was the final catalyst that led to me joining the Metropolitan Police Service in London a few months later.

Lessons learned:

- If something looks too good to be true, it probably is
- People who are unwilling to share the story of their success may have something to hide."

JESSICA HODSON: "I started working within the Financial Crime Recruitment market about a year after my arrival to London.

The moment came about after meeting someone in a pub (very London of me!) where I met a woman who was working in financial crime and she started to tell me about her role.

The conversation really did blow my mind, firstly because I couldn't believe financial institutions had internal "police teams" (my initial thought of what they did), and secondly just how enthusiastic she was about it. Who cares that much about their job?!

Question 1: "How did you start your Financial Crime Fighting career? What inspired you to take this course in life?"

It certainly was one of those lightbulb moments in life. I'm not certain why it clicked so much or why it diverged my life path so quickly, but I am certainly glad it did.

On reflection, I think it could have had something to do with the type of people in the space. In the U.K., London anyway, is known for being a bit aloof but people in Financial Crime Compliance seem to have this energy and passion for what they do. For many, it is an equal part vocation and career.

If I were to take a look back at my early tentative steps into the market, I could say with confidence it was the warmth and conviction of those early people interactions which sparked an equal passion and interest in me."

DR. WILLIAM SCOTT GROB: "I did not have plans for a career in anti-financial crime. When I graduated from university, I entered an analyst program for credit analysis.

At that time, the focus was on learning about operations, settlement, financial statement review, ratios, and customer behavior. It was the early 1990s, and the financial sector was most concerned with defaults.

While financial crime has always existed in the financial sector, the financial sector never paid much attention. This area was the domain of law enforcement. Enron was one of the first instances where fraud and default showed the growing magnitude of white-collar crime.

At the time, there was not a career track for financial crime professionals. My journey included various roles in finance from operations, credit, collateral management, risk management, structuring, relationship management to compliance. The entire time, there were multiple threads in each role that related to anti-financial crime elements. The anti-financial crime responsibilities must be across the entire financial institution at all levels.

Everyone commits to fight financial crime. Unfortunately, some people do not recognize the duty. They may focus on profit above all else. Their view espouses maximizing profits and shareholder value. While many companies have this goal in their metric, it is an incomplete goal because it ignores the more significant financial crime issues.

In 2001, the world changed with the World Trade Center bombings. The USA PATRIOT Act significantly elevated the fight against financial crime and terrorist financing when mid-town and later downtown. There

Question 1: "How did you start your Financial Crime Fighting career? What inspired you to take this course in life?"

13

was a recognition that payment systems were the financial gateways for organized crime and terrorists.

My pivot to becoming a financial crime fighter came in 2008. I arrived at the structuring desk creating exotic derivatives that provided leverage to individuals and funds. In mid-2008, the financial markets began to unravel. The collapse highlighted a vast number of frauds and Ponzi schemes such as those by Petters and Madoff. As the last person standing, I needed to unwind the portfolio of more than $4 billion, finding on my way more financial discrepancies, frauds, inappropriate transfers, and criminal actions.

Such financial crimes can destroy people's lives. In some cases, it robs them of dignity. Many anti-money laundering professionals work long hours behind monitors looking for suspicious activity.

Unfortunately, the role can be unrewarding. The lack of recognition and emphasis leads many to incomplete execution. We need to move from liability management roles to financial crime-fighting.

I was attracted to a role in ACAMS because I felt I could make a difference. Various non-profits, such as the WWF, Traffic, Mekong Club, Polaris, and OUR, have inspired me. In human trafficking and child endangerment, the criminal prey on the vulnerable and weak. At ACAMS, we want to empower individuals to go above and beyond the simple acts of know-your-customer requirements or transaction reviews. By digging deeper into transactions, we can trace the financial footprints behind these criminal syndicates. Anti-financial crime compliance has become increasingly sophisticated at detecting illegitimate sources of funds. By joining together with a shared commitment to fighting crime, we can combat the trading of people's souls. It takes a community."

MEL GEORGIE B. RACELA: "I started fighting financial crime as a financial investigator at the Anti-Money Laundering Council (AMLC), the country's Financial Intelligence Unit (FIU), from 2002 to 2008. I was part of the pioneer Bangko Sentral ng Pilipinas (BSP) staff assigned to the AMLC Secretariat upon the enactment of Republic Act No. (RA) 9160 or the Anti-Money Laundering Act of 2001 (AMLA).

Then in 2008, I was given the opportunity to head the Anti-Money Laundering Specialist Group (AMLSG) of the then newly reorganized Supervision and Examination Sector (SES) of the BSP. This group is tasked with ensuring that all BSP-supervised entities (BSPSEs) comply with the AMLA through onsite and off-site examination. With this mandate in mind, the AMLSG, under my helm, undertook the following:

- Established the first-ever risk-based and comprehensive anti-money laundering (AML) regulatory framework, i.e., BSP Circular No. 706 dated 5 January 2011, for compliance by all BSPSEs;

- Rolled out said BSP Circular to more than 1,000 BSPSEs in the country;

- Developed the first-ever AML Risk Rating System (ARRS), which, in gist, is a complex supervisory tool to determine the robustness of BSPSEs' AML compliance framework by assigning a rating of four as the highest and one as the lowest;

- Crafted the Revised Examination Manual for Anti-Money Laundering and Combating the Financing of Terrorism Activities (REMACA) for observance by all BSP examiners; and

- Launched the AML Training Course, which covered BSP Circular No. 706, ARRS, and REMACA to train and educate all BSP examiners for a sustained and consistent implementation of the regulations.

In 2015, as the Deputy Director/Officer in Charge of the Office of Supervisory Policy Development at SES, I further honed my management skills in producing macro-prudential policies, including the Liberalization of the Entry of Foreign Banks and the Minimum Capitalization of Banks. I also led the Special Projects and Reports Group that is in charge of drafting periodic reports to the Monetary Board, the most significant of which is a semestral report submitted to the Congress of the Philippines and the Office of the President, pursuant to the provisions of the New Central Bank Act.

On 1 February 2017, I was designated Officer in Charge of the AMLC Secretariat, and after six months, I was appointed by the Council to be the Executive Director of the Secretariat.

In the year 2000, I was a young lawyer working at the Office of the General Counsel and Legal Services and had my first exposure to AML. The Financial Action Task Force's (FATF) imminent directive to its members was to impose countermeasures against a list of Non-Cooperative Countries and Territories (NCCT, also known then as the blacklist), including the Philippines. I was part of the team tasked to formulate the first Anti-Money Laundering Bill for consideration by the Philippine

Question 1: "How did you start your Financial Crime Fighting career? What inspired you to take this course in life?"

15

Congress. This exposure kindled my desire to become a financial crime fighter."

JAIKUMAR (JAI) RAMASWAMY: "Before entering the private sector, I had been responsible for prosecuting a wide variety of criminal conduct with the United States Department of Justice (DOJ), including various types of fraud, cybercrime, and money laundering offenses. My experience at DOJ was incredibly rewarding and allowed me to appreciate the degree to which illicit financial activity is an essential facilitator for various organized grand criminal activity, terrorism, grand political corruption, and hostile state actors.

These activities are fueled by an illicit financial system every bit as sophisticated as the formal financial system, and that hides in plain sight by mimicking legitimate financial transactions.

Financial institutions play an enormously important gatekeeping role in preventing and detecting illicit financial activity. Compliance failures can compromise the effectiveness of the system that we have created globally to combat it. However, during my time at DOJ, it becomes increasingly clear that enforcement can only be part of the solution - it is as important for financial institutions to create the right culture to support a financial crimes compliance program.

I became a financial crimes professional to help drive the institutional change necessary to support a healthy culture of compliance."

ABTAR RANDHAWA: "My first memories of really understanding what Financial Crime meant was during my childhood and growing up in a family of sole traders. My father and uncles would set up retail outlets at various community markets across the U.K during the weekends. These were well-organized and labor-intensive drills and hard work! I recall an incident when on a spate of weekends, counterfeit currency was being used to purchase retail garments across multiple vendors. As the word got around, the police and local market authorities were informed, and eventually, over the coming months, multiple arrests were made. I recall the information provided by the local constabulary on the complexity of the events and how organized crime rackets were targeting the highly intensive cash transaction marketplace due to a lack of sophisticated tools to detect and prevent the use of counterfeit notes.

Counterfeiting and organized crime had become so severe that a special surveillance operation was set up, and global investigations and arrests were conducted to capture the ultimate ring leaders. This really awakened my senses to how serious and complex criminal activities operated and how challenging it was for law enforcement agencies to identify, record, evidence, and prosecute criminals for their illicit activities. The thing that also stuck in my mind was the victims of these crimes who were unaware of the scale and complexity of what was unfolding just by innocently accepting counterfeit notes."

ANTHONY NAPPI: "I have always known that governance and control are important parts of all businesses. History is littered with companies who failed to manage business growth and control. As Warren Buffet said, it takes a lifetime to build your reputation but minutes to destroy it.

You can have the best year financially, but one significant control break, whether that be AML, fraud or another event, negates all the positive work that was done.

When I was the CEO of the Asia Transaction Banking business, I was the first to build a governance and control team, incorporating Financial Crimes. I ensured my business managers and control teams worked closely together, and our goals reflected the importance of having a strong control environment.

If you look at the number of penalties that financial services companies have paid since the financial crises, it is well over 300 billion dollars - a staggering amount. But the impact of the dollar amount pales in comparison to the reputational impact the industry has suffered. Additionally, the regulators have become much more aggressive in oversight and monitoring and in levying large fines on companies that have violated regulation and law.

With tens of thousands of clients, it was important to have a best-in-class program that allowed us to know our clients, manage and vet their transactions and work with our colleagues across the bank in the onboarding and continual monitoring of our clients."

GUILLERMO HORTA: "My career in Financial Crime Fighting dates back to the early 2000s, as a few months after I joined one of the largest Banks in Mexico, which was at that time recently acquired by a US global Bank. As part of such acquisition, the Bank was in the process of develop-

Question 1: "How did you start your Financial Crime Fighting career?
What inspired you to take this course in life?"

17

ing and implementing an in-country AML Program up to enterprise-wide standards. AML Regulations were quite limited in Mexico, so the Bank had a big challenge of raising its bar even though more flexible controls were applicable for the rest of the Mexican Banks. During those days, it was common that the Compliance and AML Departments were part of the Legal Department. The AML Unit was mostly focused on identifying suspicious transactions, conducting regulatory reporting, keeping up to date a simple AML Program Policy and providing annual training to the 1,400 branches of the Bank.

The 9/11 attack, the subsequent uphill of controls derived from the USA Patriot Act and the results of an onsite review conducted by the Federal Reserve Bank changed the overall picture of the Compliance & AML Program across the firm. Changes were made across the Compliance and AML Departments structure, and the General Counsel for Corporate Banking was appointed as the new Compliance & AML Head for Mexico. He was a tough, strong and extremely intelligent lawyer. Even though I was not reporting directly to him while I was working in the Legal Department, we established a very good relationship. He was a very aggressive lawyer and probably even a frightening character across the leaders of the Bank, but he was exactly what the existing environment needed. A strong and solid leader who could change the overall Compliance & AML culture across the firm and the power to move all the pieces and improve the overall applicable controls. As part of that adventure, he was asked to select one member of the Legal Department that he would like to bring to his Compliance & AML Team. Surprisingly, he chose me. So, there I was, reading every available book, article and industry document that existed on the AML space, trying to absorb the foundation of AML while helping him and other Compliance experts revamping the firm's overall controls.

I started as the Head of the Compliance & AML Regulatory Unit. Two years later, I was appointed as the Chief AML Officer for the whole Bank in Mexico, and the story began!"

PAUL (PADDY) O'HARA: "It started by accident, as so many careers do. In 2000, I was a Fraud Investigator at JPMorgan, and as AML wasn't a real focus of banks then, we provided the AML training for the bank. Someone in Credit (who then performed KYC on clients) saw one of my presentations and asked me to take over the Due Diligence team. 9/11 struck soon after, and the focus on AML and Sanctions began. Combine this with a previous Police career and a strong sense of right and wrong, and I can't think of a better career to have fallen into!"

CARLOS GARCIA PAVIA: "My incursion into the Financial Crime Fighting field was completely unplanned, almost accidental. After the turn of the century in the year 2000, when the Y2K remediation projects were coming to an end, and the world realized that no real havoc came out of the so-called "Y2K bug", I made the transition from supporting good old fashion IBM mainframe technology to then deploy and support the first Regional Data Warehouse running on Oracle RDBMS (Relational Database Management Systems, perhaps a term that the Big Data generations of today may not have heard of before, jk).

From there, I started to work on other Oracle, UNIX, mid-range systems, something that I genuinely enjoyed as I was a Unix, C++, C-Shell programmer by trade, accidentally turned onto a COBOL, CICS, JCL, OS370 programmer by the need in the past. I remember it drove me crazy when people identified me as a Mainframe programmer; I immediately jumped up to clarify that my core skills were Unix and C++.

Anyway, back to the story, in 2005, after running a major program for the migration of the mainframe legacy back-end systems to mid-range for Citi's corporate bank in Latin America, I had to choose between moving to Sao Paulo, Brazil, or staying in Fort Lauderdale, knowing that I would probably not have an assignment in the short term. I decided to stay, and God was faithful (yes, I am a Christian) to open the door for me to take over the I.T. support for a small application running in mid-range known as Global Interdict.

This application was there, almost forgotten, sort of a check the box thing to run something called sanctions screening. I did not really know anything about it at that time, but this application was providing services to all countries in the region through on-line/real-time interfaces operating through MQ-Series (a. k. a. IBM web-sphere) and also processing batch files received overnight. Then, I learned that this application was used to do something called fuzzy matching against a list published by OFAC, a list known as the Specially Designated National's list. All of these were foreign concepts to me at the time.

Little by little, I started to understand that this application was of the utmost importance for the safe operation of the bank. When I realized that what I was responsible for in Citi LATAM was the ultimate line of

Question 1: "How did you start your Financial Crime Fighting career? What inspired you to take this course in life?"

19

defense to prevent the misuse of our financial network by bad actors such as drug traffickers, terrorism organizations, sponsors of weapons of mass destruction, totalitarian regimes, and corrupt politicians, then it became clear to me that the mission was much more than just providing I.T. services for an almost forgotten piece of software in the mid-range infrastructure. The mission at hand was to ensure the continuous availability and effectiveness of the screening program to prevent the penetration of illicit parties into the global Citibank network.

This automatically gave me a new purpose, something I could relate to after witnessing the events of 9/11 and the devastation that corrupt politicians and drug trafficking cartels had left in Mexico, my home country. I immediately felt that my team and I were on the battlefield, entrusted to use the best of our skills and resources to fight in the war against terror, organized crime, and corruption by attacking them where they suffered the most in their finances. Yes, it was the time for us to be as disruptive as possible to deter these bad actors from thinking about using our financial network to benefit their illicit businesses.

But this was not the first time that I was involved in a role of that sort. Back in the mid-'90s, after the financial crisis that devastated the Mexican economy, I was allocated to write COBOL programs to search for certain names of individuals and entities across the bank's systems to identify and report every account, contract, and transaction where the targeted individuals and corporations were involved. The results were astonishing, and we were able to uncover valuable information that led to the prosecution and arrest of a sibling of the former Mexican President. After following the case closely, I felt a true sense of fulfillment for the first time, knowing that the work that I had done helped to put a very high-profile corrupt politician behind bars.

At about that same time in the mid-'90s, my team and I were commissioned to write programs to identify and report transactional activity totaling ten thousand dollars or more on any given day. Little did I know that what we were writing at that time were the first rudimentary controls to prevent Money Laundering. Those reports were used by an Internal Control unit to run investigations and report findings to the regulatory entities in Mexico. A couple of years later, this unit became the first Financial Crime Compliance department in LATAM. Now, after many years in this space, I understood that since the mid-'90s, God prepared me to do this job. He prepared my heart and my thoughts to passionately love what I do, to feel that great sense of fulfillment when the fruit of our work leads law enforcement agencies to successfully ceased organized crime rinks or bring down totalitarian regimes or disrupt terrorism financing.

Fast forward to 2005, when I took over the support of Global Interdict in LATAM, I decided to get to know everything about the application and give it the visibility and importance that it deserved. I started by learning the application from the inside out. I memorized the entity-relationship (E.R.) chart of its Oracle database, and then one by one, I learned how the different shell scripts and java programs work. By late 2005 I got to know the application probably better than the Polaris Labs consultants that provided application support services for it at that time. Then, with a little bit of marketing creativity, I named my team the LATAM Sanctions Solutions team and even created a nice logo to identify it. I then toured the region, evangelizing the Compliance departments on the use of Global Interdict.

In 2006, I spent most of my time collaborating with the Global Sanctions Compliance team in the definition of a global strategic plan for screening technology. Long story short, Global Interdict became the backbone of the global screening platform for Citi, now known as CitiScreening".

Question 1: "How did you start your Financial Crime Fighting career? What inspired you to take this course in life?"

21

How can you apply these lessons and insights to your career or life today?

_____

_____

_____

_____

_____

_____

_____

_____

_____

_____

_____

In your eyes, what is the most difficult part of your job as a financial crime fighter?
How do you handle it?

QUESTION 2

TADEO (JUN) CLARAVALL: " I'll focus my answer to this question on the personal or 'soft skills' difficulties and challenges I faced in executing my role as a financial crime fighter.

The difficulties and challenges I faced as a financial crime fighter were different at each stage of my career due to the level of knowledge, experience, and maturity I had then vs now.

When I began as a junior investigator, my biggest challenge was the confidence to face up to senior colleagues. I felt I didn't have the skills nor the requisite knowledge to debate and challenge them on cases. As I got more practice and experience, I got better at doing this.

When I moved up to a mid-level management position and was given the responsibility to personally train all 5,000+ employees of JPMorgan in the Asia Pacific on Anti-Money Laundering and Sanctions, my biggest challenge became the ability to effectively engage in meaningful Q&A with the business and operations on what then (circa 2003) was still an emerging area of regulatory compliance. How do I make them see how the tactical controls they are performing tie into the bigger picture strategic risks and how everything we do or don't do has implications towards real-world criminal or terrorist activity? Again, the more I did this, the better I got at it.

When I moved to Citi and then Bank of America (circa 2010 to 2019) and held senior executive positions, the most difficult challenge was influencing other senior executives. It's an entirely different ballgame at this level of seniority as you're generally working with the brightest, most strong-willed, and savvy professionals in the organization. The ability to quickly and effectively simplify the complex nature of financial crime risk and programs to influence them to take or refrain from taking specific actions and decisions was a crucial skill I needed to develop. As with the earlier challenges I listed, the more I practiced it, the better I got. But the practice wasn't enough because I needed to get better faster, so I had to get timely coaching and mentoring from others who were much better at it than I was.

In all, I'd say that the most significant challenges I faced in my career as a financial crime fighter have always been in the area of soft skills. Skills that required additional knowledge, practice, and experience to address.

The key for me was not to be afraid or even when I was afraid. To just do it anyway, try and fail and try again, was essential to overcoming my difficulties.

Another key was having a trusted coach or mentor, someone who has been there and done that was a secret weapon not just for me but for many others that I know of who have done and achieved noteworthy things in their careers."

MARTA LIA REQUEIJO: "Political perspective: The most difficult part of my job is being aware of the human and environmental impact financial crime has and realizing so much more could be done if there was the will.

Take as an example the transparency on beneficial ownership; we all know how critical it is, we all know where the "issues" are, but we need governments to take action.

We have enough anti-money laundering, tax, and terrorism financing standards; governments now need to focus on effectively implementing and enforcing those standards.

Operational perspective: To appropriately prioritize, manage expectations of senior stakeholders and build a team with the right skills, it is critical to understand the business vision and strategy.

When implementing and maintaining effective financial crime systems and controls, it is crucial to balance what very often are conflicting objectives:

• Ensuring a proportionate approach to the firm's specific financial crime risks
• Enhancing operational efficiency and effectiveness
• Limiting the negative impact on customer experience
• Ensuring readiness for scaling the business

Awareness and communication are also key; you need the business's buy-in, and to achieve that, you need to successfully 'sell' the idea of compliance. This means being able to work collaboratively with the business and present 'the financial crime world' in a narrative consumable by non-financial crime experts."

PATRICIA SULLIVAN: "The core parts of financial crime fighter include

1) Helping the bank and our clients deploy effective strategies to prevent and mitigate the use of our services by bad actors, so we keep the doors of commerce open to the good guys, and

2) Provide useful information to law enforcement to support arrests and prosecutions and ideally asset seizures.

Unfortunately, when you are performing any leadership role in a large corporate, you will have to manage the job's administrative and political side, which is often time-consuming and not necessarily in service of the mission. As a leader, I put a lot of effort into shouldering this aspect of the job for the team, so they have more freedom to focus on fighting financial crime."

JOHN FOGARTY: "On reflection, the answer to this question changes the more senior in an organization you become. As an Analyst or Advisor, you may struggle to piece together all the information and make sense of the data to draw an inference or conclusion. As a leader, galvanizing a large team behind a common purpose and keeping them motivated under internal and external pressure with varying priorities is often challenging. Open communication is key to success at all levels. Transparency builds trust - whether asking a peer or colleague for advice, seeking an opinion from a mentor, or articulating a strategy and purpose to your team, no harm has come from me being open with the people I deal with."

ERIC FAVILA: "I liken my job to that of a health professional's trying to convince people to live healthier lifestyles. When there is a crisis, financial institutions pull all the stops to remediate their financial crime (FC) programs and meet regulatory expectations. In less strenuous times, it is extremely difficult to convince institutions to maintain a healthy and robust FC program. Further, institutions tend to have the view that you can set and forget FC programs. Since organized crime is always evolving and innovating, a system constantly scanning for threats and continuously improving is critical. A healthy and robust FC program has a research and development component constantly scanning the environment for emerging threats and regular diagnostics assessing any vulnerabilities arising from changes to the business model, evolving client needs, and the need to maintain competitiveness. Without this, a colleague of mine often refers to this as a battle between organized crime and disorganized banks.

It is a thankless job. Professionals in this line of work cannot afford to be wrong and let their guards down. However, on the flip side, the cost of disregarding their advice when they are right could cost jobs and reputations – a bill that cannot be measured. A former law enforcement officer once told me 'that the war on crime is a constant fight. There are no deals to be won or accolades for "good years." Just know that those who need us, know we are there fighting for them. I, therefore, take comfort that I am part of the force of good.'

In the last 2 years, I have spent considerable efforts on a crime that I feel the financial services sector has not done enough about, the online sexual exploitation of children or OSEC. I have taken a personal interest in assisting anyone needing help to navigate the complication and nuances of the payments sector when it comes to combatting OSEC. It is important to concisely define OSEC. Sexual abuse of children is not a new concept. Unfortunately, internet prevalence, affordable technology, and a global remittance network have introduced the commercialization of this abuse. When the abuse was confined to familial ties, the abuse was limited to occasional abuse. When commercialized, we now see children trafficked, repeatedly abused on a daily basis, and getting younger up to a few months old.

According to the International Justice Mission (IJM), an international NGO focused on human rights, law, and law enforcement and with a specific strategy to combat OSEC, defines the crime to be "the production, for the purpose of online publication or transmission, of visual depictions (e.g. photos, videos, live streaming) of the sexual abuse or exploitation of a minor for a third party who is not in the physical presence of the victim, in exchange for compensation."

The Philippines is the largest source of such material in the world. Combine easy internet access, cheap technology, a vast remittance network with poverty, and an international language such as English and it is the perfect combination to abuse children commercially for global consumption. There is a lot of attention towards law enforcement and technology platforms. Social media companies employ technologies to detect such activity and lead the charge in generating leads to rescue chil-

Question 2: "In your eyes, what is the most difficult part of your job as a financial crime fighter? How do you handle it?

27

dren. However, as with any commercial crime, choking the money flow is essential to disrupting the abuse. Unfortunately, the local banking sector has not stepped up. It has been a personal mission to help local law enforcement obtain quality intelligence from the local banking industry rather than relying on referrals from foreign partners."

ANTHONY QUINN: "The most difficult part has been about getting the right level of focus from regulated entities, first working for one, trying to get projects sponsored and supported when the consequences of non-compliance for years was next to zero, and then as the Founder of a RegTech business (before RegTech was a thing!) and trying to get companies, regulators and Boards to believe in what you are trying to do, to improve financial crime risk and compliance management capabilities.

For many many years, it felt like I was alone screaming down a well, with mild curiosity but frankly not much success in getting the message out of the importance of financial crime risk management and the potential implications of weak and ineffective controls.

In terms of how I handled it – this is just pure bloody-mindedness, in the face of resistance to change, being focused on the mission, and more importantly the higher purpose of what it means to society to minimize the substantial harm of financial crime on society.

Put simply persistence beats resistance, so you need tenacity, drive, and determination to last the distance and get through any adversity."

JOHN CUSACK: "If you want to make a difference, you have to be somewhere that is important and for long enough to do good work that outlasts you. This usually means understanding large institutions and the many stakeholder groups whom you need to build credibility and generate trust. Unfortunately, along the way, you will come across people who you have little professional respect (though many more that are inspiring). Still worse, these individuals may even end up for a time as your line manager or be important in a matrix organization.

Maintaining professional integrity throughout these periods is essential, and in my experience, people are found out eventually, albeit it feels a couple of years later than it should. Those years feel like an eternity, but you can still do great work and learn some important lessons, including later years when you take senior roles and remember how it feels to have experienced these periods.

We are privileged to do the work we do, are highly compensated, and have to meet difficult challenges. Yet, people make though the difference as to how we feel about all of this - happy and motivated - disgruntled and frustrated."

JESSICA HODSON: "There is one part of my role which even thinking about now makes me feel a little somber.

This is when someone has been made redundant (or even fired). In my role, I have a bit of a unique bird's eye view of the market, which is fantastic because I know when roles are coming up, I can pick up the trends and make sure I can help people in that space. However, this also means when someone calls me in tears because they have lost their job, I have the heart-sinking knowledge that their particular role isn't going to be at a high volume for a while.

I have had a lot of very hard conversations with people who feel hopeless, and only one word can cover these calls—heart-breaking.

In the coming years, these calls are going to become too common due to redundancy following the pandemic and market changes.

The only way to handle them is to focus on the things we can do. Help them with their CV, share their profile with clients free of charge or send their profile to my competitors to see if they have heard of roles I haven't.

To put it simply, the only thing to do is whatever you can do and to stay in touch as much as possible.

If someone is reading this, and you are in the awful boat of job loss–don't be afraid to "annoy" your recruiter. Stay on our radar, and if you just want to know what the market is doing, we can tell you as much as we know."

YVETTE CHEAK: "It is never easy and what is most difficult is to convince others that there may be an anti-money laundering issue in a transaction or in parties one is dealing with. What is important is to ensure you have clearly studied any transaction or issues carefully and carried out due diligence, and then convince others with the facts."

PAUL (PADDY) O'HARA: "Taking the time to be able to make a difference, not just for the Bank you work for, but society. I'm passionate about PPPs, about stopping fraudsters, human and wildlife traffickers, and it's only working as an industry and with the Police that we can hope to make any difference. Filing a SAR and exiting a client only moves the client to the next bank. We should be working with the Police to ensure they're prosecuted. Something that happens all too rarely."

SCOTT BURTON: "The most difficult part of my job is ensuring that a risk-based approach and effective AML program is provided to the Bank and customers. Balancing risk and controls to ensure the Bank is a front foot ahead of standard Regulatory compliance and also approaching risk in a commercial manner; sometimes when rules and regulations are too prescriptive and not risk-based, it can be a challenge."

ABTAR RANDHAWA: "In my role, we wear many hats and juggle many priorities all at the same time, and this all adds to the complexity. However, the primary one is protecting the customer and always keeping that ethic front and center of my daily activities. The reason being, I have witnessed first hand impact of financial crime activities on small businesses that do not have the appetite to swallow any setbacks.

In tackling issues, the daily reality is navigating the complexity of systems, processes, and people, which doesn't always allow for the quick and easy fixes we desire. Therefore, it is imperative that the focus point of all we are endeavoring to achieve is a sustainable solution with measurable long-term attributes that also allows the organization to pivot and be agile as and when emerging risks and issues arise. One such example is an agile audit, risk, or compliance plan that is built on both industry and market intelligence metrics (including law enforcement agencies and regulators), qualitative and quantitative measures that provide forward-looking insights into exposure and early alerts and incidents that may point towards systemic and prolonged problems."

MARLENE MELI: "With my operations background, I was always interested in and focussed on operational efficiency. Whatever the process is, it should be stable, reliable, efficient, effective, and well documented. When it comes to software solutions that efficiently support financial crime fighters at banks in their daily work, the most difficult part is to translate the requirements and needs into sustainable solutions.

I often observe that I.T. specialists are absorbed with the technicalities and thrilled about the latest technology but do not really understand what the business and compliance users need to efficiently and effectively investigate alerts. What supports them to easier and faster assess whether an alert is true or false? How can they improve the quality of SARs before filing them? Hence, conducting detailed interviews with financial crime investigators, trying to understand their real needs and how well they can handle their daily tasks is crucial for a better understanding and as a consequence implement better solutions."

NICK TURNER: "In principle, the concepts are easy to understand. The regulatory environment is highly unstable. I practice in the area of economic sanctions, which changes in response to international politics.

Keeping up with the new is a job in and of itself. It's important to know when to tune in to new information and when to tune out the noise. Otherwise, it would be overwhelming."

ROD FRANCIS: "Wow, that's difficult to name just one! I've worked primarily for large global financial institutions with complex businesses, and therefore the FCC compliance program is complex. One of the most challenging aspects of the job, as a leader, is to achieve good connectivity between the 1st and 2nd line of defense – between the business (client-facing staff selling the firm's products and services) and risk management functions sitting in the second line. One of the keys to success is understanding the business, products, and services and how operationally the business 'end to end' operates. Without this, you really can't understand risk in the context of FCC or have credibility with your stakeholders, which is one of the cornerstones of building trust.

During my career, I have systematically looked for opportunities where I could expand my knowledge across different FI lines of business and products and services, including Consumer Banking (retail and cards), Private Bank, Institutional including Corporate Banking, Investment Banking and Markets, Asset Management, Investment Management, and Insurance. I'm no expert in any of these business and products and services (I've hired people who are), but I know enough to ask the right questions and add to my credibility."

JEROME MICHAILIDIS: "As someone who works in policy and training, it is difficult to constantly analyze and determine what are the most important messages for our staff and clients. It would be all too easy to simply copy/paste all information from the regulators, but we have a responsibility to interpret and transpose."

MAGGIE QIU: "The most difficult part of my job as a financial crime fighter is to influence people. In my role, it is essential to work well with internal stakeholders to gain their support and buy-in on our FCC program and controls; it is more important to gain trust and communicate effectively with external regulators, monitors, and auditors. Many of them are much more senior and often have very different perspectives.

The way I handle this is to rely on fact/data-supported discussion and effective communication without jargon. Using the actual numbers or examples to explain the FCC risks, do not say no without providing alternatives and other solutions to the issue for internal parties. I often also discuss the potential consequences as well as the value-added aspects of the matters on hand. For external parties, explain our FCC program's attributes in a more structured manner, and focus on the demonstrations of program effectiveness, avoid using jargon, and prepare the need to provide education on some basic concepts, since we cannot expect all regulators or external assurance people have the same level of understandings as us, hence patience is a must."

MARTIN JAMES WALLIS: "There are many negatives working in this field, and it can sometimes be challenging to work in the face of this when you see the impact that financial crime has on individuals and their communities. That awareness of the social impact, especially those targeted for their vulnerability, can be heartbreaking. In trying to manage this, you could adopt a clear, analytical, and unemotional perspective if you only focus on numbers bouncing around the globe. That would be an easy way to minimize the impact. However, I do think this challenge can be used as a strong motivator to do more. Keeping the social impact of financial crime in mind and trying to make a difference where you can, however small, means you create a positive to counter these negatives. This is one of the core elements I have observed across the industry, the desire to do better. This is a very unifying ideal and manifests in the discussions around best practices and knowledge sharing and keeps the momentum moving forward."

JASON HOLT: "Simply put, too much crime and not enough time!

On the one hand, one of the most exciting aspects of a career fighting financial crime is the variety. Driven by an ever-changing landscape of new criminal typologies, innovative products (such as fintech and crypto), new laws and regulations, and the changing focus of regulators, there is seldom a dull moment.

Of course, this also translates into one of our greatest challenges. How to adapt and evolve fast enough to ensure we can successfully mitigate these new risks. This is more important today than ever before, as we see the pace of change accelerate further every year. As if that wasn't challenging enough, we need to do this against a backdrop of an ever-increasing focus on the cost of compliance.

How to address this? Well, we could look at smart strategies to ensure that management understands the impact of changes and the use of pre-agreed metrics to articulate and drive resource allocation, or the need to ensure that the 2nd line of defense is genuinely focussed on their roles and not taking on 1st LOD responsibilities and reallocate roles accordingly, or to use risk tolerance thresholds to manage the volume of risk in line with resources.

These are important but ultimately tend to simply shift the resource question from one place to another or act as a brake to the business.

After much consideration, I concluded that the only way to keep pace with change is through the use of technology. AI and Machine learning are now within reach of most firms. Appropriate use of these technologies can free up valuable resources from labor intensive roles while performing these tasks far more effectively than any human could."

DR. WILLIAM SCOTT GROB: "Each year, an estimated 1 to 2 trillion dollars of illicit financial flows enter the financial system.

Organized criminals profit from narcotics, arms trade, counterfeits, modern slavery and human trafficking, environmental crime, cybercrime, fraud, bribery, and corruption. Only a tiny amount is detected. Crime is profitable.

Banks are essential to criminals because they are crucial to transferring profits. Because of the sheer volume, movements of cash are too evident and heavy. The better solution is to move money electronically with a wire transfer through correspondent networks from one country to another. Criminals can steal funds through deceptive techniques and move the funds shortly afterward to the other side of the world.

David Lewis, the Executive Secretary of the Financial Action Task Force, was quoted by GFI saying, "Everyone is doing it badly," when queried to rate the effectiveness of the global anti-money laundering fight. From my perspective, we are not fighting to win.

After almost thirty years, our efforts are not yet fully realized, despite billions of dollars of investments from the financial sector on building policies, systems, infrastructure, detection methodologies, and techniques. We need to continue to bring awareness, training, and collaboration to fight financial crime.

Our governments have failed us.

We have not enacted rules for transparency or tightened loopholes. From legislative actions on beneficial ownership to information sharing, we have been unable to protect our communities because organized criminals have used their profit to paralyze our legislative and judicial processes.

Investigations take time.

Law enforcement and prosecutors have tended to prosecute clear-cut cases. Financial crime cases are rarely straightforward. We must move from chasing the stooges to prosecuting the kingpins.

The challenge of being a financial crime fighter is to change attitudes and behavior. Our profession needs to elevate the discussion. We need to push FATF and our governmental agencies to advocate for reform. We can fight indifference and share the anti-financial crime tools and techniques, but we need modifications in existing laws and legal practices that handicap the fight.

We will continue to educate and train our industry. Moreover, we must continue to enhance the competency within and outside our profession.

We do what is right. Increasingly, our collective efforts are making a difference.

Month after month, I see individual AFC heroes hearing the call to become more deeply involved in fighting financial crime because they hear the voices of the victims."

ARMINA ANTONIOU: "I think the most difficult thing about working in FinCrime is switching off. I have found myself out shopping on the weekends and sometimes wondering, "How is that business making any money? I wonder they are a front for laundering". Life isn't all like Ozark or Narcos or other Hollywood crime shows!

That's why I love sports so much. I get engrossed in the competition and love watching and supporting my teams. I spend most weekends watching grassroots and professional sports of some description, and I very much try not to think about work.

Sport is an integral avenue for kids to learn how to cope with setbacks, deal with others fairly and respectfully, and reap the rewards of personal effort. More importantly, and as the United Nations Office of Drugs and Crime (UNODC) promotes, sport is a powerful tool to steer youth away from crime and drug use, empower minorities and promote sustainable development and peace. Even though I am switching off by watching sport, it's doing something positive for the community too!

I have also spent more time in the garden and increased my indoor plant collection – especially during the lockdown. I really enjoy seeing something that I have grown from a clipping or seed eventually develop flowers or even edible fruit or vegetables. My very limited cooking skills are now benefitting from the flavor of fresh vegetables and herbs."

GUILLERMO HORTA: "The most difficult part is the evolving risks that all financial institutions face on a day-to-day basis. Criminal organizations move at a super-fast speed. By the time Banks identify a typology and establish reasonable controls to mitigate such risks, organized crime is already finding new ways to move the money, overtake controls, and identify the Banks with a weaker AML Program, which will facilitate the disguise of illicit funds. Therefore, a financial crime fighter can't relax thinking expertise has been achieved. A true financial crime fighter keeps learning on a day-to-day basis.

Financial services are evolving faster than regulations, so the expectations of Senior Management and Regulators is that Banks should always be ahead of the risk. Not an easy task, especially for those professionals like me that work for international firms, where you are dealing with multiple countries around the world, each one with different risk exposure."

ANTHONY NAPPI: "It is important to be able to balance business growth and good governance and control – and to protect the firm, but not overburden the organization with draconian dogma and processes that add little value and are so complicated that cannot be implemented and managed.

Question 2: "In your eyes, what is the most difficult part of your job as a financial crime fighter? How do you handle it?

35

When a negative control event would happen, the natural tendency is to overcompensate with more controls, more processes, more overhead. While changes are required, more does not always mean better – so being able to improve controls while simplifying, streamlining, educating, automating and ensuring there is frequently input and communication with the entire organization so that everyone understands their role in protecting the firm, and the importance of control. This sometimes gets lost when firms overreact post a control break."

MEL GEORGIE B. RACELA: "The most difficult part of my job is how to break down the 'Chinese Wall' among law enforcement agencies (LEAs) in the country. This barrier holds true not just in the Philippines but common to jurisdictions all over the world. In fact, it took the 9/11 terrorist attacks to make the US LEAs realize this problem, address it, and correct it.

For a better perspective, we all know that money laundering is a derivative offense, meaning there must be a predicate offense before we can prosecute them. Under our existing legal framework, the AMLC is mandated to investigate money laundering, whereas other LEAs investigate the predicate crimes. If we do not establish a strong partnership with the LEAs, which can feed us with predicate offenses, we will not have anything to investigate. All the rich financial transactions in our database will be worthless.

Hence, to address this, in 2017, we institutionalized the one-year-old ad hoc arrangement that we call Targeted Intelligence Packaging (TIP). The TIP is a lock-in workshop with a particular LEA, for instance, the Philippine Drug Enforcement Agency (PDEA), where we educate the counterpart investigators and officers with what the AMLA is, what our functions are, and how we can work together. This is followed by the sharing of intelligence and re-prioritization of targets, and it concludes with the tasking of both agencies. This one-week-long activity may seem short, considering the number of cases and financial transactions involved. Still, it actually starts months before the workshop and continues until the final conviction of the subject for both money laundering and the predicate offense of drug trafficking, as well as the forfeiture of all proceeds of said crimes.

These workshops have proven to be fertile ground for various cases, culminating in the freezing and forfeiture of multiple accounts and other properties worth hundreds of millions of pesos that involve numerous subjects and filing complaints about money laundering. But more than all these, equally important is that not only are we able to gain the trust and confidence of our counterpart LEAs, but we are also able to establish close relationships with them. By doing this, we do not have to worry about the 'Chinese Wall.'"

CARLOS GARCIA PAVIA: "Perhaps the most difficult part of fighting financial crime is to balance the effectiveness of the compliance programs and the ability to operate with minimum customer friction. This becomes even more important in the world that is becoming more and more digitalized every day.

Users of financial services through digital channels want to have frictionless apps that allow them to do what they need to do immediately, without delay or unnecessary steps. While this is all reasonable customer expectation, the reality is that financial institutions have a moral and societal obligation to safeguard the integrity of the global financial systems and doing that requires additional information and time-consuming verifications.

All financial institutions are mandated to operate under a strong control framework that is ever more demanding to prevent the infiltration of bad actors that may misuse the financial network to operate their illicit businesses. Achieving the needed balance is incredibly challenging, but it is undoubtedly required to ensure that the traditional brick and mortar financial institutions remain competitive against the increasing number of virtual financial services challengers, who are much more nimble and agile in their operation than the blue whales of the global financial markets.

The battle for supremacy in the digital era is fought through data and analytics. Organizations capable of acquiring, maintain, and process high-quality data throughout their operation will be the winners if they also invest in the analytical capabilities to extract the insight that will deliver the right intelligence to automate their Compliance processes as much as possible. It is here where the use of Artificial Intelligence and Machine Learning (AI/ML) technologies is vital, but its outcome will only be as good as the data that is ingested. Hence, the first step is first enhancing the quality of data and having proper data governance in place is perhaps the most important step to achieve the goal.

Now, there is a caveat in all of this. We can have the cleanest and more insightful data in the world, being processed through the most sophisticated and smartest of the AI/ML technologies, but if we cannot explain the process in layman terms to anyone who is not embedded in the process, then it may be worthless. What internal or external reviewers of these processes want to see is that we, the Financial Crime Risk Analytics (FCRA) and Financial Crime Compliance (FCC) professionals, understand and can explain in clear detail how our processes work, what are their key controls, how they are monitored, how they are governed and how we know that they are effective. Failure to achieve this may lead to disastrous consequences ranging from bad ratings to hefty penalties to cease and desist orders, depending on the magnitude of the findings.

While it is true that large financial institutions are subject to more stringent regulatory regimes, smaller financial institutions should not relax their efforts to run top-notch Financial Crime Compliance programs. After all, it only takes a good, experienced reviewer to knock at the door and find out a small crack to then uncover a whole crater in the process. Sadly, this has brought some small community banks and credit unions to an end in the past few years.

Some of these unfortunate organizations did not see the risk coming to their businesses when some bad actors were being kicked out of larger banks as part of their de-risking strategy. Those bad actors decided to move their financial assets to smaller financial institutions knowing that these did not have the astringent levels of Financial Crime controls that larger institutions have.

Even non-financial services companies like Amazon have suffered the consequences of not having sound screening controls in place. Just a few years ago, Amazon spent millions of dollars to fortify their screening processes and to look back at millions of orders through several years to identify and report potential violations to U.S. Sanctions Regulations.

The new virtual financial services disruptors in the market are no exempt from having strong, effective, and efficient Financial Crime Compliance programs. There is no reason for these emerging players to run their businesses with a risk appetite that allows a disproportionate level of risk for their organizations. It is here where the market disruptors will be in a leveled field with their larger competitors to achieve effective Financial Crime Compliance with minimum customer friction."

How can you apply these lessons and insights to your career or life today?

_____

_____

_____

_____

_____

_____

_____

_____

_____

_____

_____

_____

Do you have a unique or interesting financial crime fighting story that you can share?

QUESTION 3

TADEO (JUN) CLARAVALL: "Too many to count. Here's one that happened early in my career, which left a deep impression on me.

Our team reported a set of transactions to a country regulator and F.I.U. (Financial Intelligence Unit). Our bank was an intermediary bank that received cash letters (USD denominated cheques) from an Ordering Bank's client to clear through the U.S. clearing system. This transaction involved multiple cheques, sequentially numbered, of the same large amount and totaling a substantial sum. The ultimate beneficiary was a prominent high-ranking politician in that country. This SPF wasn't too bright, allowing large funds to go to an account in his name.

Many months later, I saw on the news that a corruption investigation was launched by law enforcement on this politician for allegedly receiving bribes for the exact amount we reported. This politician vehemently denied the allegations of corruption and denied receiving any such amounts. I remember watching this on T.V. feeling a deep sense of satisfaction that our work was making a difference. Sadly, this politician passed away sometime later before justice could be served.

This event left a strong imprint on me as a young financial crime fighter. It taught me that what we do truly matters. It matters because the information that we pass on to regulators and law enforcement could lead to the arrest and conviction of bad actors in society."

YVETTE CHEAK: "I do have but am not able to share as I am still bound by the Official Secrets Act."

JASON HOLT: "Early on in my career, I discovered what appeared to be a large-scale fraud, with the associated money laundering taking place alongside it.

The firm that appeared to be the victim was looking at potential losses of up to USD 250 million (pre-financial crash, that was a lot of money!).

Question 3: "Do you have a unique or interesting financial crime-fighting story that you can share?"

41

The matter first came to my attention as a result of the victim firm (A) noticing that its client (B) had suddenly ceased to make repayments on their loans. In addition, as had all the third parties (C), to whom the client B had sold goods.

At the same time, A's well-respected external auditor had resigned. Interestingly, noting in its resignation that they had based this at least partly on concerns arising after requesting B's, clients (C), to confirm the transactions they had carried out with B. A sharp-eyed auditor had noticed that the confirmations they received all came from the same fax number, rather than separate from each of the counterparties C, which they would have expected.

My investigation commenced. Shortly after, I discovered negative news about persons associated with B; this exposed that they were under investigation in Asia for VAT fraud, arising from the false representation of items being shipped between jurisdictions. Shortly after, I also discovered that there were connections between B and its customers C that indicated they were not indeed at "arm's length" counterparties.

These connections included some common shareholders, shared addresses and contact numbers, high use of Hotmail style email addresses, and more common than would have been expected use of the same banks. Moreover, other connections with payments flow from a sister company were identified that raised additional concerns.

I began to express my concerns to management at firm A, arguing that this all looked highly suspicious and needed to be investigated further. However, as soon as my suspicions were raised that this could be a more malicious matter than a simple credit issue, some members of firm A's management became increasingly aggressive and unwilling to consider the concerns and suspicions that had been identified. In fact, this grew to such an extent that at one point, after a particularly challenging meeting on the topic, I was pulled into a side meeting room by a member of the line of business' senior management and informed, in no uncertain terms, that, they could and would get me fired if I refused to stop raising these malicious and unfounded concerns about their client.

With a law enforcement background, I was threatened with career criminals' far worse consequences than being fired. With the support of my own leadership and firm A's most senior management, I persisted with my inquiries.

As the investigation progressed, the case developed into an interesting and relatively complex one.

Firm B was principally a physical commodity trading firm that had obtained loans from A to finance the purchase and sale of commodities. Firm A had also provided facilities to allow 3rd parties C to finance the purchase of commodities from firm B, usually for a term of 180 days. They were allowing sufficient time for the goods to be shipped from B to C. The commodity in question was designed to act as the security for A if any counterparties defaulted. This aspect is significant, as A believed it was able to manage its risks by hedging against price fluctuations in the commodities, always believing they had good security over the physical goods. The trading activity of B also indicated they were a successful and properly functioning business.

Unfortunately, investigations revealed that despite firm A's initial representations of the high status of the warehouses, where the commodities were allegedly held (from which they took significant comfort), they were not in fact of that standing. Worse, it was apparent that an employee of the warehouse had been compromised and had allegedly falsified documentation (sadly, this individual died while the investigation was being conducted).

Further, examination of the letters of credit (L/C) associated with the export of goods from B to C revealed more issues, including sequential L/C numbers (which would be unusual for separate shipments) named ships that were not in the ports stated at times stated, ships that we're incapable of transporting the goods said or were unsuitable for doing so.

It was further noted that B also had the facility to raise payments directly through their own bank, including adding details of the originators, thus giving the appearance that funds were being emitted from the third parties C when in fact they were not.

Finally, on the investigation of payment flows, it became apparent that B had been receiving significant funding from a sister company based overseas and that these funds had originated from similar loans granted by other banks to them, also based on bogus assets and documentation.

When looked at based on macro payment flows, it became apparent that little, if any, external funds had come into either business, but that the funds seen were in the main based on bank loans which were obtained and then used to pay off loans granted to the sister company and vice-a-versa, all the while hiding these flows behind a veneer of false documentation, designed to give the appearance of a legitimate trading business.

Ultimately, law enforcement acted, and a number of individuals at B were arrested and convicted of fraud, as were members of management of the overseas sister company.

Firm A lost over USD 200 million as B had allegedly lost all the money borrowed trading on the commodity markets."

MEL GEORGIE B. RACELA: "For the past five years in waging the "war on drugs," the government has gained significant success both on the supply and demand sides.

For the demand side, we have seen a substantial decrease in drug users from the estimated four million drug users in 2016 to the current estimate now at 1.7 million (2020 estimate of the Dangerous Drugs Board), or a 57.5% success rate. Not to mention that all large illegal drug laboratories have been paralyzed and demolished.

Relative to the supply side, the AMLC has caused the freezing and filing of forfeiture cases on over PhP3 billion in bank accounts and assets. If used to manufacture prohibited drugs, these funds can be multiplied by 10fold to 15fold or equivalent to PhP30 billion to PhP45 billion. The Philippine National Police (PNP) and the PDEA have seized drugs and equipment worth a total of PhP40 billion. Hence, with our combined efforts, we were able to deprive drug traffickers between PhP70 to PhP85 billion worth of drug proceeds, approximately 15% of the estimated four-year gross revenues of PhP560 billion.

What interests me the most about this war is that we can immediately see and feel its success, and we are proud to be a part of it for the benefit of the youth, the future of this country.

But, of course, this is the big picture. There are specific stories, too. Consider the following:

- Drug Trafficking

In 2017, PDEA requested the AMLC to conduct a financial investigation on a certain man arrested during a buy-bust operation of PDEA. An estimated amount of one kilo of methamphetamine hydrochloride (shabu) worth PhP2,000,000 was seized from him. In addition, financial documents, including handwritten notes, checkbooks, and deposit slips to nine individuals, including a certain company, were recovered during the buy-bust operation. The man was subsequently charged with the violation of RA 9165 or the Comprehensive Dangerous Drugs Act of 2002, as amended.

Based on the AMLC's initial financial investigation, numerous large-denominated transactions of the subjects had no underlying legal or trade obligation, purpose, or economic justification because the subject persons failed to substantiate the veracity of their transactions with financial documents. There were abrupt increases in the number of transactions made to the different bank accounts of subject persons and entities, beginning in 2016. Moreover, the nature of the businesses owned by the subjects could not justify the sudden increase in the amounts transacted and the volume of transactions to the accounts of subject persons.

Consequently, several suspicious transaction reports (STRs) were filed with the AMLC pertaining to the transactions of the subject persons and entities. Investigations conducted by the banks revealed that said transactions were not commensurate to the respective financial capacities of the subjects.

There were identified transfers of funds with no established relationship between the parties to the transfers. Transfers of funds were also noted with persons and entities who are respondents to civil forfeiture cases relating to the violation of RA 9165, as amended, filed by the AMLC with various courts. Thus, this further taints the accounts with proceeds of illegal drug activities.

In 2018, an AMLC resolution was issued, authorizing its Secretariat to inquire into the bank accounts of the subjects. Subsequently, the Court of Appeals issued a freeze order against those bank accounts, involving over PhP670 million in the accounts. The AMLC is in the process of its bank inquiry into the subject bank accounts for the filing of a petition for civil forfeiture on the funds if warranted and the filing of a money laundering case against the subjects.

In addition, the initial investigation disclosed that the proceeds of funds were channeled to a sole proprietorship engaged in the online selling of luxury bags. Observed were numerous large-denominated cash/check deposits and local fund transfers among the subjects, which mainly originated from Fujian, China.

- Online Sexual Exploitation of Children (OSEC)

Question 3: "Do you have a unique or interesting financial crime-fighting story that you can share?"

45

The AMLC is aware that child pornography has become one of the rampant and emerging threats in the Philippines. The country has been tagged as the "global epicenter of the live-stream sexual abuse trade of children," as stated by the UNICEF in 2018.

This crime, however, is not bounded by territorial jurisdictions.

The AMLC conducted a study in 2019 titled "Child Pornography in the Philippines: An Evaluation Using STR Data (2015 to 2018)." We identified approximately 3,000 persons of interest (POIs); and revealed the modus operandi, which includes the fact that the country fills the supply side, while nationals of more advanced economies feed the demand side; and typologies for covered persons to guide them in identifying potential OSEC transactions.

The AMLC study on child pornography paved the way for the creation of the Information Exchange Working Group of the Egmont Group on child sexual abuse and exploitation (CSAE), bringing together the United Kingdom Financial Intelligence Unit, Australian Transaction Report and Analysis Centre (AUSTRAC), and the AMLC as project leads. The Egmont Group is a united body of 166 FIUs, and it provides a platform for the secure exchange of expertise and financial intelligence to combat money laundering and terrorist financing.

Using the AMLC study as the primary source document, the working group completed the "Combatting Child Sexual Abuse and Exploitation through Financial Intelligence: Project Report," producing a consolidated list of financial indicators and keywords that financial intelligence units can use to identify financial transactions likely to be linked to the online streaming of CSAE. Said study has been shared with more than 160 countries and now the subject of ongoing investigations of LEAs in all corners of the world.

Inspired by the success of the first study, we updated the same to cover the period 2019 until the first half of 2020. This second study resulted in the identification of more than 23,000 POIs. We have received many requests for information from various foreign jurisdictions, seeking to obtain more information about the perpetrators and victims. While this is an ongoing task not only domestically but also internationally, we have seen arrests happening all over the world, which effectively disrupts the facilitation of said crime."

MARTA LIA REQUEIJO: "In the earlier stages of my career, I have experienced the unfortunate situation of reporting financial crime risks and issuing recommendations that have not been appropriately followed through by senior management. When facing a similar situation, it is of the utmost importance to do the right thing for the firm and you and to live up to your ethical values. When things go wrong, always do the right thing."

MATT FRIEDMAN: "In November 2018, I traveled to Washington, D.C., to attend the American Bankers Association's (ABA) Financial Crimes Enforcement Conference. As a counter-trafficking expert, I was invited to participate in two-panel discussions focusing on the issue of modern slavery and the banking sector. Following the second session, one of the bankers came up to me and told the following story.

Three years earlier, he was traveling with his family across several states in America by car to meet up with relatives. After a long drive, he pulled into a small motel off the highway. Because it had been a long journey, his wife and two teenage daughters felt tired. That evening he went out to get some food for the family. As he was coming back to the motel, he noticed this very young teenage girl being pulled into a room with an older man. He said he remembered she had such a sad, frightened expression across her face. He knew immediately what was about to happen – she was about to be used by this patron. Since he had daughters of his own around the same age, he felt he needed to do something to help.

After dropping off the food, he went to the motel manager and told her what he saw. He then returned to his room, not knowing if anything would happen. Twenty minutes later, there was a police car parked in front of the room. Ten minutes after that, he saw someone being taken out in handcuffs. The young girl was escorted to another car and driven away.

He said he remembered this event because he felt so good that he was able to help this young girl out of this terrible situation. In fact, he went on to say that this was a major milestone in his life – something he felt very proud of.

After hearing his story, I asked him what he did for a living. He said he was a compliance officer focusing on anti-money laundering for one of the major American banks. I asked him if they did work related to the issue of modern slavery. He said yes, but they were just getting started in this area, and that was why he came to the session. He went on to say

Question 3: "Do you have a unique or interesting financial crime-fighting story that you can share?"

47

that he felt his job was not very exciting and he wasn't sure how much difference it was making.

Throughout the world, many people in banking compliance do their jobs, not realizing that the outcome of their work could have a major, positive impact on our society. Over the past two years, human trafficking continues to emerge as an important issue within the banking sector. With an estimated $150 billion generated from this illicit crime annually, banks must ensure that none of this illegal money makes it into their business. If it does, and regulators find out about it, the bank can be fined for money laundering.

Therefore, many banks are stepping up their efforts to track this crime. This includes training their employees, breaking down crimes into component parts to identify potential links with banking procedures, using "red-flag indicators" to search their data for nefarious activities, and, if found, sending this information to financial regulators.

With this in mind, I told the ABA banker in front of me that while his day-to-day efforts might not seem as dramatic as his motel encounter, there were many people who could be assisted through his work in the coming years. I went on to say that those involved are our future heroes because what they are doing will help to protect not only their bank but also many other people like that teenage girl. His face brightened. I was surprised that he hadn't understood this before.

I have told this story to many bankers. What amazes me is that many of these people don't make the connection between the important work they do and the enormous value it adds in potentially helping people out of exploitation. For some, this simple story offers an epiphany.

Here is another story I often tell. It shows another reason why I have been so involved in this work.

During the time I was in Nepal, I started visiting shelters that took in trafficking victims. The best way to understand the extent of an issue is through the eyes of a person who has experienced it.

Below is a translation of a letter I received from a young girl named Meena. She was trafficked to India and endured the brothels for several years. She had AIDS. I received her letter the day after I visited her at a shelter in Kathmandu. The depth of Meena's anguish can be felt in her words. Many other victims have similar thoughts and feelings that are never revealed to the world. This offers a glimpse into their broken hearts. Read these words carefully – they hold a very important message.

"Matthew,

Thank you for your kindness in coming to see me yesterday at the shelter. Your words brought great joy to my broken heart.

I turn 15 on Monday. After being used by so many men, I can see that my days will soon come to an end. My illness gets worse with each passing day. I can hardly eat. The food has no flavor. It is sour like so much of my life. I will not see my sixteenth birthday.

I look back on that day when I left my family's home. I was only 12 then. I was so happy. So full of life. I had such hopes and dreams. Now, look at me. I will never marry. I will never have children. I will never have grandchildren. I will not grow old.

The day that first man took my virtue was the day my God died. He and all those other men stole my life away. I was just a child. Why did nobody come to help me? I have stopped asking why this happened to me. I have even stopped feeling angry.

I need you to promise me. I need you to do what you can to prevent any other girls from falling into this hole. Promise me you will end this evil. Promise me you will never stop trying. I don't care about myself. I'm done. Don't let any more of our sisters go through what I went through. My spirit is already dead inside. My body will soon catch up.

How can this happen to a child? Where are all the good men? Where are our protectors? Where is our humanity? Promise me.
Meena

I read and re-read this letter at least 20 times that day, with tears streaming down my face. Many of us who work in this field are driven by these passionate pleas. This is one of so many. This young girl was only 15 years old. She was commercially raped more than 7,000 times.

Question 3: "Do you have a unique or interesting financial crime-fighting story that you can share?"

49

There are literally millions of women and girls in this situation. Meena asked two important questions: "Where are all of the good men? Where are our protectors?" They are out there. We just need to find them, wake them up, and help them to work alongside us to combat this problem.

Reading this letter so many years ago was another epiphany that helped me to understand that we, the citizens of the world – collectively and individually – have a mandate to help end the suffering of those like Meena. Human trafficking represents one of the most disgusting human rights violations of our time. To address this problem, I realized that we needed to establish a "second-generation abolitionist movement" in which we all step up and do our part. English abolitionist William Wilberforce and others led a movement more than 150 years ago.

So can we. For human trafficking to end, we must care. We must all care."

NICK TURNER: "I spent a year helping to carry out an AML and sanctions look-back and compliance remediation project for a regional bank based in California.

The bank had a weak AML program for the better part of a decade. You can imagine the things we found. That's where I learned that money laundering is easier to spot than you'd think, and there's a difference between unusual activity and truly suspicious activity.

I took the opportunity to learn the bank's products inside and out and volunteered to draft the bank-wide risk assessment.

I still use this knowledge today. Then, I came to Hong Kong and started a new adventure doing sanctions compliance in one of the most diverse and exciting regions in the world."

JESSICA HODSON: "Ah I wish I could share some of the more salacious gossip stories which I hear but one of my all-time favourite stories is actually a lot more interesting!

Many years ago there was a senior FCC Manager within branch of a well-known bank in South America. She had a reputation for being firm but fair and had been trying her hardest to instil a strong compliance culture.

She had the unusual challenge of facing strong pushback from people who felt afraid. This woman and her team had been threatened by people who were being prevented from using the bank for untoward purposes.

Not only did she not step down, she went and worked in the branches to support her teams there.

I always recall this story as a great example of someone who really had a passion for the work she did, and at the same time was comfortable leading by example – not to mention brave!"

ANTHONY QUINN: "Not sure if this is all that interesting, but I remember going and visiting some large, regulated entities in the gaming sector probably 10 years ago and was told by Senior Risk Executives: "Thanks for showing me your system, all this issue tracking is great and everything but frankly we can count on one hand the issues we need to track".

With an independent inquiry underway into that sector, as well as major non-compliance issues also in the financial services sector, they clearly had more issues that they should have been worried about back then – might have saved them a fortune!"

JOHN CUSACK: "Plenty but if I told you, I'd have to… put it this way Robert Maxwell, Sani Abacha, Vladimir Montesinos, bin Laden, the Vatican, Oligarchs, Adeboli, the Gupta's and big incidents involving Russia, China, India, Iraq, Iran, Sudan, Myanmar & North Korea to name just a few were all part of the rich tapestry of life-fighting financial crime."

MARLENE MELI: "In February 2016, when there was the terror attack at Brussels Airport in Belgium, a close workmate of mine was almost one of the heavily injured victims. He was on the way to the airport for a business trip, and literally just minutes before he arrived there, the bombs exploded. I was at that time in Washington D.C. to present our software to a high-profile audience when I learned about this devastating news. For me, that was a kind of turning point.

What I did in fighting financial crime till then was important from a moral, ethical and legal point of view. But since this terror attack, it became close and personal. Whatever I can do to stop the financing of these attacks, I will do.

Although this may sound like very big words with little impact, I do believe that it is our mutual obligation to fight financial crime wherever and whenever it occurs and whatever is needed to do so."

Question 3: "Do you have a unique or interesting financial
crime-fighting story that you can share?"

51

ABTAR RANDHAWA: "During my time as an Auditor for a major European Airline, my primary role was ensuring the safety and security of our staff and passengers. Given the complexity of multi-jurisdictional rules and regulations coupled with the nation-state/nationalistic identities pertaining to the status of a particular flag carrier coupled with historical, cultural nuisances, the role of forming a single view on an action plan to address risk was a challenge given that any perceived weakness in control could be seen a direct challenge to the sovereignty of the state.

One such incident occurred where our procedures had picked up a live and possible terrorist threat to the airline. Without going into the sensitivity, it was critical that immediate and decisive decisions were made using evidence and well thought out scenario analysis that had agreement from multiple stakeholders. Various authorities, including diplomatic services, counterintelligence services, local and international ground handling agents, and senior management, were required to be briefed on a 'real-time' basis. The threat of terror and the financing of terror-related activities showed me that the rationale for performing such barbaric acts was and could also be political. This instilled in me a clear view that financial crime in whatever form it takes (and is usually global in nature) and the motives of criminals provides me with enough justification to do my best to instill counter financial crime activities to hinder, prevent and eliminate the threat these individuals and groups pose of society."

GUILLERMO HORTA: "Absolutely. Probably two of the most important stories in my life. The first one, working as Chief AML Officer for an international Bank in Mexico City. It was early in the morning, and I was getting ready to go to the office while listening to the morning news. Suddenly, I hear the anchor-man informing the audience about suspicious large cash transactions reported by my Bank as a SAR regarding a PEP running for a Presidential candidate. I was clearly aware of such a report as I was the individual legally responsible for such submission to the authorities. Still, I would never imagine seeing the actual physical image of my SAR on TV...

My heart stopped for a second, I ran near the TV, and I was shocked when I was even able to see my name at the bottom of the document. The complete SAR was right there as if it was a public document that could serve as evidence to destroy the political career of such a candidate. I immediately got concerned about my safety and rushed to my office to start a full strategy on managing such an unpleasant event.

Back in those days, unfortunately, it was very common to find out that the content of SARs filed by financial institutions was leaked to the press for political purposes; what I recalled demanded an infinite number of discussions between Mexican Banks and local authorities.

The second story was probably four years later.

One day before Christmas and just on my way to leave for the Holidays, my assistant picked up a phone call received in my office from an individual who strongly insisted that it was urgent to talk to me about a personal matter. After three attempts, I finally agreed to take the call. To my surprise, the individual identified himself as a member of a Mexican Drug Cartel who wanted to warn me about the "damages" we were causing to his business as a result of our duties. He immediately told me where my father lived, where my sister worked and how they supposedly had gunmen outside of my apartment ready to take my daughter and her nanny, as well as other gunmen following my wife who was at that specific time at a nearby supermarket. I don't know how but I figured out the way to keep him talking and called my wife immediately, who surprisingly confirmed to me that she was, in fact, at the alleged supermarket. My legs started shaking, and I immediately grabbed my cell phone and called my boss in NYC to inform him about the situation. Corporate Security got involved, and long story short, from that day on, a police car was parked day and night outside of my building, bodyguards were assigned to my family and me, and it was the way of living in Mexico until I was finally able to move to the US with another financial institution."

MAGGIE QIU: "My unique story is about my elevator Pitch. It is a story of how I landed my China MLRO job. On a spring day of 2010, I arrived in the office early.

When I stepped into the elevator, my big boss-Global Head of AML, was also there. After saying good morning, I decided to do a mini-pitch about myself and what I wanted to do next, all while in the elevator. I told him I worked for him in the FIU team doing data analytic and modelling for detecting suspicious transactions, mentioned progresses on some of our projects, and then went on to talk about how I wanted to explore opportunities to bring me back to China so that I can be closer to my mother. A few days later, he called me into his office, mentioned the China MLRO post just opened, and encouraged me to apply.

After a lengthy interview process, I eventually got the job. This was the beginning of my financial crime-fighting experience in Asia.

When I looked back, I think the 2-minute self-promotion exercise we did in business school really helped. I managed to find the courage and content to carry on the elevator pitch - turned an often-awkward moment to effective networking."

ANTHONY NAPPI: "Most organizations spend more time in self-flagellation mode than celebrating the many successes that occur. When a problem arises, everyone is engaged, and pandemonium sets in, but something good happens; it's simple falls between the cracks.

While I was the Chief Administrative Officer in Asia, I recall a situation where a prospective client came into a branch and wanted to move money to the Iranian Embassy. The branch staff knew this could be a potential issue and raised it to our regional Compliance team, who first thanked the staff for escalating the issue and then instructed them not to move forward. When I found about this, I spoke to our Compliance team and then to the Chief Country Officer, and we decided to all go to the branch and present an award to the branch staff who stopped this transaction and to the branch manager. We did a short presentation and award ceremony and spoke about the importance of governance and control and escalating issues when you have any uncertainty.

We then published this event on the company website, and I strongly feel that thanking and rewarding people for doing the right thing helps build a strong culture of control."

ROD FRANCIS: "Again, a very difficult question as so many stories over the years that one would have are confidential, often dealing with Investigations/SARs. Dealing with regulators, particularly from a US and China perspective, and law enforcement, including DoJ re Sanctions risk decisions related to China-related clients, was interesting. It was a great example of how Governance and Oversight are critical. Equally, it highlights the importance of having the correct risk decisioning framework in place with the correct people making reasonable risk decisions that are well documented. This protects the firm but also protects you as an individual."

CARLOS GARCIA PAVIA: "February of 2011. A new sanctions program against Muammar Qadhafi's regime in Libya was about to be enacted through an Executive Order awaiting to be signed by the then-President Barack Obama. Through an unparalleled collaborative effort, Sanctions Compliance Officers across multiple financial institutions in the U.S. and abroad were scanning diverse sources on the internet to identify persons and entities closely related to the regime. Overnight, a list of potential targets to be searched across customers, contracts, and transactional records was gathered. The objective was to identify and freeze the financial assets that the Libyan regime had scattered around the world across multiple institutions.

Right after Executive Order 13566 was signed, we triggered the screening processes to run right before the opening of the financial markets the next day.

The result was an outstanding success. Billions of dollars were frozen, giving no opportunity for the Libyan regime to react and move those assets out of the reach of the financial institutions mandated to comply with U.S. Sanctions Regulations. The feeling of fulfillment was exhilarating. Yes, we spend the whole night gathering intelligence to win this battle, and we did. Not even one of us complains about lack of sleep or tiredness in the process. That faithful night in February 2011, we were all working together in unity, sharing and analyzing the information gathered from the open-source. We were all focused on doing our best to gather reliable and actionable data to trigger the most effective hunt for the Libyan financial assets. We all knew that we had only one shot at doing this effectively. Failing to do this would have given the Libyan regime the opportunity to react and move their assets into hiding, but that did not happen. Not long after this operation, the ruthless regime of Muammar Qadhafi came to an end."

PAUL (PADDY) O'HARA: "Not specifically but going back to PPPs being the only way we can combat financial crime, we've been pushing FIUs and regulators across the region to start them. One is KoFIU in Korea, who I've met several times to talk to them.

Last week I was told that they want to start a PPP and are now looking for a model that will work for them. Such awesome news; makes me realize that these continual conversations are worth having, and we can be part of making a society that little bit better. It wasn't just me; FATF direction has helped!!! It doubles your resolve to keep working on the FIUs of other countries!"

Question 3: "Do you have a unique or interesting financial crime-fighting story that you can share?"

55

How can you apply these lessons and insights to your career or life today?

_____

_____

_____

_____

_____

_____

_____

_____

_____

_____

_____

_____

_____

_____

What do you think is the
most effective strategy to
fighting
financial crime?

QUESTION 4

TADEO (JUN) CLARAVALL: "In my experience, from a financial institution's perspective, the most effective strategy to fighting financial crime is to ensure that every effort expended, every dollar spent, and every decision made in their fight against financial crime is geared towards achieving three main goals; namely, (1) to ensure compliance with the letter and spirit of the law, (2) to ensure that relevant and meaningful reports of suspicious activity are made to regulators and law enforcement promptly and (3) to the extent permitted by law, share information, learnings and other relevant intelligence via formal and informal public/ private or private/ private partnerships."

JOHN CUSACK: "Once we define and agree on a definition of "Effectiveness" relevant to each stakeholder group and all stakeholders are pulling in the same direction to the same ends, then we can talk about successful strategies. From an FI's perspective, I recommend reading the Wolfsberg papers on Effectiveness. For greater insight than I can provide here. In addition, check the work of the Global Coalition to Fight Financial Crime."

ANTHONY QUINN: "Any financial crime risk management strategy needs to start with the basics and, that is a thorough understanding of the risks and vulnerabilities of businesses to financial crime by performing a comprehensive enterprise-wide money laundering and terrorism financing risk assessment.

Only once the ML/TF risks have been identified, assessed, and clearly understood can the organization turn its collective mind to developing a control framework that is both appropriate and proportionate to the risks that they might typically face in an attempt to mitigate and manage them.

Unfortunately, we have seen that many regulated businesses do not understand their ML/TF risks and, therefore, any strategy to combat financial crime might be misguided or overlooked rendering it ineffective."

MATT FRIEDMAN: "Based on our experience working with financial institutions related to modern slavery, we have come up with five steps that we consider essential. They include: 1) providing detailed awareness-raising information to both the leadership and the compliance officers; 2) assisting in the development of internal policies and procedures for addressing modern slavery; 3) developing a set of typologies to map criminal activities and related transactions found within a given geographical location; 4) based on these typologies, identifying which of these transactions could be red-flag indicators for nefarious business activities; and 5) packaging these red-flag indicators to search big data for possible modern slavery activities. Since most financial institutions follow this same set of steps for other crimes (e.g. drug trafficking, wildlife trafficking, counterfeit goods, etc), integrating these procedures within ongoing efforts is generally not a problem."

YVETTE CHEAK: "Proper Training, not just to know the law but to understand different methods criminals use to prevent detection and sharing with other practitioners."

JEROME MICHAILIDIS: "I think it requires constant attention to details of regulation, listening to industry practice, and focus on your respective institution's risk culture."

NICK TURNER: "There's a difference between activity that looks unusual because it lacks context and activity that is truly suspicious.

A good financial crimes strategy, in my opinion, is one that focuses on the real red flags and closes out the easy cases as quickly as possible.

It always aggravates me when a bank spends too much time checking boxes for what is obviously a low-risk activity when there are more interesting cases that need skill and attention applied to them."

MARTIN JAMES WALLIS: "No one person can do this alone. Therefore, it has to be a collaborative approach, something we have been trying to help deliver on with the great work of the FinTech FinCrime Exchange, bringing like-minded individuals together to share typologies and best practices in the fight against financial crime. If we don't collaborate, criminals will always stress test and find the weakest links and exploit it to maximum effect through repetition at scale. Our current thinking has gotten us to the system we have now. One element to highlight is the way

Question 4: "What do you think is the most effective
strategy for fighting financial crime?"

59

individuals and corporates use legitimate schemes to bring tax efficiencies using corporate structures, these can be abused by criminals for illicit purposes, as shown by the Panama papers and other exposés, so I would also suggest that greater transparency needs to play a part in any effective strategy."

PATRICIA SULLIVAN: "After significant trial and error over the years across people, process, and technology, I have a strong view that the private sector will only succeed in identifying and stopping significant financial crime issues by working in legal frameworks that support proactive intelligence sharing B2B and public sector to private. The supervisory frameworks must likewise recognize and credit private-sector intelligence-sharing efforts and de-prioritize work that does not yield meaningful information to law enforcement. The case has been made through pilots in the US and UK, but the legal and supervisory frameworks to support are lagging."

DR. WILLIAM SCOTT GROB: "The most effective strategy for fighting financial crime is a three-pronged approach:

- Understand and prioritize the mission.
- Assign a senior manager as the steward.
- Empower middle management.

It is not enough to announce a project, outline some tasks, and hope the organization will collaborate. I think the book titled "The First 90 Days" by Michael D. Watkins can serve as a guide for many.

First, we need organizations to prioritize financial crime with mission statements and senior management leadership that activate staff and resources.

Signaling from the top is essential at the start. It provides guidance, alignment, and the message about the destination and needs. You need senior management to convey the priority and urgency of the mission.

Organizations that have explicit signaling execute the best. Many banks have a strong internal culture of resisting change to protect the financial system from rash decisions. The need to address anti-money-laundering deficiencies may run counter to this embedded culture.

Second, it is not enough to get senior management and board statements, key performance indicators, policies, and risk appetite statements.

It is essential to drive these goals into middle management, where execution will happen.

No organization has unlimited resources. Tasks may land on one function or an individual unable to drive the entire implementation. You need a senior steward accountable for the execution, which has the gravitas to make the change. Without this steward, the project will become mired with delays.

Third, it is necessary to hire or train professionals with the proper crime-fighting skills. Do not assemble the group without a clear understanding of the required internal capabilities to address the inherent risks. Putting the wrong leaders or hiring inappropriate people at the helm demotivates staff.

In my experience, when you get alignment in the three areas, you get urgency, momentum, and action. These three qualities lead to an effective strategy for fighting financial crime.

When only one quality exists, I have witnessed unintended consequences from senior leaders as they straddle business and compliance objectives at odds."

JOHN FOGARTY: "Within a large organization? Put simply – "Data, Data, Data" Clean, accurate, and assured data from source systems cannot be underestimated. It is the foundation of all programs to fight financial crime. I have undertaken many remediation programs at large Banks, and this is the one area that is so simple to say yet hard to achieve. Process automation and capability can all be built around effective data management."

MEL GEORGIE B. RACELA: "I do not intend to represent our strategy as the most effective, but what I can assure you is that by doing 'ECC,' we can attain success. These are as follows:

Educate. There are limits to what we know and what we can do in the same manner that there are limits to what other LEAs know and can do. So, we need to build our capacity through education because, as Malcolm X once said, 'Education is the passport to the future, for tomorrow belongs to those who prepare for it today.' Hence, we educate ourselves by partnering with various FIUs, which already have established systems and processes to learn from their best practices. With the help of multilateral agencies, we hired consultants to assist us in formulating our own manuals and training modules. In formulating the training modules, we actively participated and suggested topics so that trainings will be specific to the AMLC setting. To be specific, AUSTRAC has trained all our analysts because analysis of big data is common to all FIUs. A veteran investigator guided the formulation of our Intelligence Analysis and the Financial Crimes Investigation Manuals. The US likewise invested in our investigators and lawyers through training on effectively investigating and prosecuting terrorism financing. These are just a few of our ways to hone our financial crime-fighting skills.

But then again, if those trainings and skills only remain with the AMLC, it will also be useless. Thus, we try our very best to offer trainings to our LEAs so that, in turn, we can increase their awareness not just on the legal, regulatory, and procedural framework but also the typologies employed by criminals and the best practices employed by other jurisdictions to fight crimes. By doing this, we can open lines of communication, and, with it, we hope to start a long-standing relationship with them.

Collaborate. With a message that we have a very rich financial intelligence, the necessary skills and training to investigate, and a recognition of the limits of what we can do, we make it very clear that we can do more together. By collaborating, we can reach a state that is greater than what we can do individually. This cannot be truer than a one-nation approach, where all agencies, LEAs, and otherwise, contribute to a common goal.

Commit. Like the first two, this is also a continuous process. We continue to educate and learn, collaborate, partner, and commit until we see the fruits of our labor, depriving the criminals of the profits of their crime. By repetitively doing ECC, we strike criminals where it hurts the most: their proceeds of crime, their sources of funding, illegal assets, and financial transactions. Ultimately, this maintains the integrity of domestic and international financial systems and decreases lawlessness, thus protecting the common good.

The observance of the ECC strategy holds true not just in our role as the country's FIU and as reliable law enforcement and prosecutorial partner (as a matter of fact, our TIP, which is based on this ECC approach, does all these things), but also in our performance as an efficient supervisor of covered persons.

Alongside law enforcement, supervision, through the issuance of regulations, validation mechanisms, and, whenever possible, a public-private partnership, plays a very important role in financial crime-fighting. It is believed that involving the private sector is equally critical because the fight against financial crimes starts with prevention. Under this particular scheme, the front-liners are officers and staff of covered persons: the board of directors (BOD) and senior management because they set the tone of compliance culture; and the team because they are the ones that deal with customers and implement the AML and counter-terrorism financing (CTF) regulatory framework in their respective institutions. The robustness of the covered person's AML/CTF framework is only as strong as its compliance culture and the integrity of front-liners.

Even in the area of supervision, we still apply the ECC. We raise their awareness through trainings and sharing of intelligence products to both our co-supervisors and covered persons; we collaborate with them by setting a common goal; and we commit to the achievement of a common goal."

ARMINA ANTONIOU: "I have always adopted an outcomes focussed way of working.

If all financial crime fighters are truly focused on the outcome of identifying and mitigating financial crimes, rather than simply following a process, then we would all be more effective. A flawed process won't help to stop criminals plying their trade, and we won't necessarily realize our processes could be improved if we don't also focus on whether the process is achieving the outcomes we intended."

PAUL (PADDY) O'HARA: "Proper functioning PPPs, where the FIs and FIUs are true partners."

ROD FRANCIS: "I'll address it from a broader ecosystem perspective, and if we do so, we can focus on many aspects, but to me, the main issue is:

Better Public/Private partnership – improvements have been made worldwide in several jurisdictions in the last ten years – UK, Australia, and Hong Kong as examples. However, much much more still needs to be done.

The partnership between governments/regulators, law enforcement, private sector – FI's and NGO's is still not effective. Information sharing has improved but is still lacking and not good enough. As an example, I'm currently undertaking some pro bono work that involves online

Question 4: "What do you think is the most effective strategy for fighting financial crime?"

63

child exploitation. I am working with a law firm, NGO, and the industry, and I have spoken to several regulators.

A very difficult subject and unfortunately prevalent and easier to perpetrate based on the plethora of payment processors (FinTech's that have entered the market) and new channels such as crypto that now exist. Are FI's aware of this as an issue? What information exists from law enforcement and NGOs that could be used by FI's to help in the fight? What are regulators doing to prevent criminals from using new channels such as PI's of Crypto to facilitate such offenses vs. total reliance on the banks with banking licenses and interface with the financial system?

Compliance Culture - I see many examples of it already in the public domain. I've seen now, particularly as a consultant, how bad the compliance culture within financial institutions can actually be. From a financial crime compliance perspective, we run a program because underlying risks affect real people. We are trying to help guard the financial system against bad actors, and ultimately, we're trying to give good intelligence to law enforcement.

Some people who work within financial institutions don't care much about that. They don't really have the right mindset and the right culture within them to want to comply and do the right thing. Part of our role is trying to prevent that kind of poor compliance culture because it undermines our efforts."

GUILLERMO HORTA: "Staying ahead of criminals. Adapting and constantly enhancing our Financial Crimes controls, making sure our program is agile and constantly reviewed to reflect the reality of the services and products offered, the footprint where we do business and the risk exposure of each financial institution as a result of its way of doing business."

ANTHONY NAPPI: "From a strategic perspective in building a solid process to prevent Financial Crime and other control events, I believe the following is very important:

1. "Tone from the Top" – the firm's senior leadership must lead the control and governance process – they must make it a key pillar of the firms' strategic priorities and part of the management discipline.

2. Communication and shared goals and responsibilities – everyone in the organization must be part of the control process and must understand their role and responsibilities. Additionally, educating the client base as to what is expected and why it is important to protect them and the firm.

3. Three lines of defence – firms must have three lines of defence to protect the company – strong first line ownership and control review and vetting – strong second line teams – Compliance – Legal as an oversight and challenge process in addition to being subject matter experts to help guide and support the first line and a strong third line Audit function to review and challenge that the controls are adequate to safeguard the firm.

4. Education and Training programs that all staff must take to understand the various aspects of governance and control – financial crimes and be empowered to appropriately discharge their responsibilities.

5. Investment in tools, technology, automation.

Ongoing and open and honest discussions with the regulators."

ABTAR RANDHAWA: "There is no single strategy to fighting financial crime as the nature and complexity of globally organized criminal activities go deep into society. However, the one principle that can enable us to achieve meaningful goals is working closely with all relevant regulatory bodies and law enforcement /intelligence authorities to not only enable us to be informed and undertake inspection related activities but to also provide a fair challenge to the desired approach to eliminate any meaningless tasks or obstacles in the process.

I have witnessed the agility and resources criminals have at their disposal. Therefore, providing an adequate level of counter-crime fighting also requires the same level of nimbleness and tenacity. Fortunately, our industry has created a vast database and depth of knowledge, intel, and protocols that would render many counter financial crime activities meaningless without this knowledge. Sharing of information, best practices, risk, compliance, and auditing approaches, and identifying emerging risks across industry and amongst our peers is a key critical component to aiding a globally accepted strategy to fight financial crime. What my life experiences have taught me is that although one may think the counterfeit notes being used to purchase merchandise was an opportun-

Question 4: "What do you think is the most effective strategy for fighting financial crime?"

65

ist trying his luck, what is most likely the reality is much murkier and a real threat to the pillars of society."

CARLOS GARCIA PAVIA: "I would say that the strategy to effectively fight financial crime is to ensure the continuous flow of timely and current actionable intelligence to efficiently alert on potential financial crime activity as early as possible.

To execute this strategy, it is essential to have the right data at the right time, the right analytical capabilities, and the right talents in the right locations under the right governance and control framework. This combination of essentials is the driver to enable more predictive capabilities in the Financial Crime Compliance (FCC) programs.

The FCC programs of today are mostly reactive; an event that seems to be suspicious, or the execution of an unusual transaction, or a match against a watch list trigger an alert after any of these things happened. Millions upon millions of these alerts are generated every year, most of them being completely unproductive. Then, these alerts are either passed through post-detection filters for triaging or are directly delivered to Operations for adjudication. These Operations teams are then left with the task of finding the needle in the haystack. It is here where most of the cost of Financial Crime Compliance is, an ever-increasing cost for the past few years.

And then, the COVID-19 pandemic in 2020 brought tremendous disruption to these reactive FCC programs in the form of unexpected changes in transactional behavior. Everything that we programmed in our old reactive Transaction Monitoring and transactional fraud prevention systems, the way we trained them and tuned them up, came to be useless. Nobody anticipated the dramatic changes in transactional behavior that completely disrupted the generation of alerts in the process. This brought these systems back to square one. New scenarios had to be identified, thresholds had to be adjusted to reduce the noise while trying to make sense of the new behaviors and learn again what was important and what was not.

But what if we do it differently? What if the FCC programs were capable of using available intelligence to proactively highlight potential bad actors or illicit activity? What if the FCC programs evolve to be intelligence-led rather than being behavior-driven?

Of course, there are particularly important ethical considerations for the FCC programs to evolve in this direction. The right data must be used in the right way to prevent our systems from automatically making biased decisions. The right data governance must be in place to ensure that data is current, reliable, consistent, and accurate through the end-to-end processes. The data must be used from and within the right locations to comply with the data privacy regulations of each jurisdiction where the financial institutions operate. The right talents must be in place to ensure that the right set of skills is available to properly manage the different aspects of each of the FCC and FCRA programs. The right governance and control framework is needed to ensure that each component of the process is properly and continuously documented, controlled, monitored and validated to remain as effective and as efficient as possible."

REFLECTION

How can you apply these lessons and insights to your career or life today?

_____

_____

_____

_____

_____

_____

_____

_____

_____

_____

_____

_____

Do you believe there is more that
we can do to fight financial crime?
If so, what more?

QUESTION 5

TADEO (JUN) CLARAVALL: "There's certainly more we can do from a regulatory, law enforcement and private sector perspective. But I will address this question from the perspective of Financial Institutions and specifically those working in the second line of defence.

We need to upgrade the knowledge and skills of financial crime fighters working inside financial institutions. Specifically, up-skilling soft skills and technology skills.

Many practitioners I know have solid technical, financial crimes capabilities but appear to lack the accompanying leadership and influencing skills to make change happen. A typical example of this is when a Financial Crimes Risk and Compliance Officer needs to influence management to, as an example, invest in upgrading financial crime systems when there is no explicit regulatory requirement for it but is necessary to make the program more effective and prevent future problems.

This person's ability or inability to communicate effectively and influence appropriately could spell the difference between having adequate systems and controls to identify and report money laundering or inadequate systems, which might lead to missed red flags resulting in missed opportunities to report suspicious activity.

As for technology skills, I don't believe that Financial Crime Fighters need to have skills to start coding A.I. systems; instead, they need to think like a coder, applying logical and data-driven thinking to understand these new technologies better and fully leverage them. Another important consequence of thinking like a coder is that they can assess how these technologies could be misused by criminals to perpetrate financial crimes or circumvent the financial institution's controls."

JOHN CUSACK: "Of course, there is more that can be done, but there is also less. What's important is to find the right balance. We should be doing more of what makes sense and less of what doesn't. Before we can do this, we need to define effectiveness and agree on what the common purpose is. We can then promote and incentivize those actions that lead to measurable successes and retire or reduce those areas that don't. For example, it would be too easy to differentiate more and better understand the differences in criminal financial activity with over 20 different predicate offenses to money laundering and take a regional and or country approach rather than a global approach as the profiles and red flags may be different. It would also be easy to say to staff up an FI FIU that proactively targets financial crime using intelligence and advanced analytics. It would be easy to say invest in greater online tools to focus increasingly on fraud and cyber-enabled fraud proceeds and conduits. It would also be easy to say you should try to increase information sharing opportunities through current legal and regulatory obstacles limit many. All these new areas of interest are laudable, and I regularly promote them all and more besides. I do, though, with the caveat that to do more should come with a change in the current approach if Banks are to be judged only on what they missed and not also on what they have found.

If technical compliance is more important than fighting financial crime and if a zero-tolerance approach is preferred over a truly risk-based one, then the imbalance militates against doing more. That's not where I'd like us to be, and that's why doing more cannot be divorced from doing less, though that's not an option open to Banks under the current regime."

ERIC FAVILA: "As with most things in life, there is always something more that we can do to make the world a better place. Whether it is climate change, race/gender equality, or global hunger, we can always do more.

Combating financial crime is no different. There is no debate about the societal impact of financial crime. One aspect where I believe more can be done is the relationship between regulators and in the industry it supervises. There is fatigue in the relationship between regulators and financial institutions. Often regulations are viewed as a burden on corporations – limiting opportunity and innovation. Especially in good times, when money is flowing, it is human nature to lose sight of the bigger picture. Regulation is the backstop to save the industry from itself. Regulators, however, also have a lot of opportunities to engage and enhance the relationship. They've been accused of not understanding the industry and being constantly on a fishing expedition to find fault. The game of cops and robbers was probably appropriate in the past. With growth, sophistication, and awareness it is my hope that the relationship between regula-

Question 5: "Do you believe there is more that we can do to fight financial crime? If so, what more?"

71

tors and industry also matures where they actively collaborate to improve the economy and prevent financial crime in a sustainable manner."

YVETTE CHEAK: "Of course, there is much more to be done. Criminals are getting smarter. They know what you are doing to put in the controls, and they try to circumvent them. So never be complacent but stay alert and develop an eye to see-through schemes and a nose to smell out fishy transactions."

JOHN FOGARTY: "This is not a static environment in which we operate. As criminal networks evolve, so should how we look to identify, disrupt and deter financial crime. Information sharing is always critical in effective deterrence but somewhat limited in most jurisdictions through legislation. As a result, organizations can only see and act on the information available to them, which may only be a small piece of the puzzle. By itself, it may not amount to any worthy examination, but the larger puzzle could be critical in completing the picture. Consequently, we need to continue to find ways to share our data across institutions safely and securely while meeting all our obligations."

MARTIN JAMES WALLIS: "I don't think anyone can stand up and say that there isn't more we can do to fight financial crime. Like many complex problems, a multi-pronged approach is required. Many of the current efforts could be considered reactive, dealing with identifying and stopping the movement of illicit funds after crimes have been committed. Like any network, if we disrupt this upstream, it negates further work along the criminal's value chain. I think that we should look at some of the instances of why crime is committed and where. Working on such key issues such as global poverty, health and corruption would impact this and limit the operating environment for criminals at the source and minimize the reasons why some individuals become involved in the world of crime. There are organizations out there that are involved in this, but this must have a commitment right at the top as a nation-state activity. It is not just an issue for financial crime but has multiple benefits by improving global equality across the board. If COVID-19 has taught us anything, it is that we can rally around a unifying problem."

MATT FRIEDMAN: "In many ways, the financial sector is just beginning to scratch the surface of fighting financial crime related to modern slavery. For us to have more of an impact, we need to increase awareness of the importance of this topic. Once sensitized, more financial crime fighters need to be enlisted to use the red-flag indicators to search for nefarious activities within big data. Because this is a relatively new topic, few banks have started to do this. But with fines and penalties increasing related to this topic, it is becoming a reputational risk for those institutions that ignore this topic."

JESSICA HODSON: "I will always come at this type of question from a people and talent perspective. While there is great diversity in financial crime, we still face a predominantly white leadership level.

I appreciate this is probably more to do with the industry and is a hard one to tackle, there is a lot to be said for only having one homogeneous lens looking top down at financial crime for a whole sector, and results this garners.

I believe different life experiences will lead to differing interpretations, and views of financial crime. This should mean, in theory, that the more perspectives you have available, the more likely you are to see the problem and solutions – particularly when combating financial crime globally.

It is interesting, as a industry, financial crime has a great diverse group of people up until VP level, but it is rare to see a minority lead leadership board, which is disheartening at times.

I spend my career placing incredible, talented and dedicated people into great roles and it is sad and frustrating to acknowledge the journey to the top will be easier for some.

The pool of talent in financial crime is there, but for one reason or another it fails to push through the glass ceiling past the VP level, or at least not with the same ease others can.

The talent in an institution is the one thing which can genuinely set it apart, so if there is something which should be done, it would be creating pathways to ensure a more diverse team to help fight financial crime at the top."

ABTAR RANDHAWA: "Yes, by being agile and flexible to keep abreast with the ever-changing landscape and by developing more accurate data analytics. Organizations are now recognizing this and prioritizing getting the right level of data surveillance and threat modeling in place, which in my view, is critical to identifying trends and patterns early on. Basel regulations and regulatory fines and penalties on lack of integrity of data have corrected organizations' ways of collecting, analyzing, and using data. This has forced perfection on many organizations to have critical data elements and data traceability at the forefront of their initiatives to improve measurement and metrics of their organization's transactions."

WILL BROWN: "An organization's talent strategy is a key weapon in its financial crime-fighting armory. As a recruitment professional, I believe it's the most important aspect to achieving more within Financial Crime Compliance departments. While this will be dependent on the budget, a pro-active hiring plan should be a part of any overall organizational development strategy.

The people hired will determine the approach to fighting financial crime in any business. They will help to dictate the internal culture relating to FCC in addition to any external regulatory pressure that the specific institution is under. An FCC function must also be given a strong platform internally; otherwise, it will be subject to limitations and frustrations. This platform is set by the people in a business, particularly the C-Suite, who will set the tone of the communication, both formal and informal.

With the waxing and waning of external regulatory pressure on each financial institution dependent on where they are in their regulatory lifecycle, e.g., underactive consent orders, DPA's, etc., trending towards BAU, the size of FCC functions will also be subject to change. Legacy growth or down-sizing in the FCC team and the current state of technology and team size play a part.

Budgetary constraints will also affect the quality of the individuals hired and, therefore, the sophistication of the techniques and capabilities of the FCC function, as well as the imagination and bandwidth to advance the fight against financial crime. A poor hire in a key role can cost the firm millions of dollars should the resultant function fail in its mission to guard against activities that results in a fine.

Advancements in the fight against financial crime will come from financial institutions who are willing to invest in the right people and technologies to support the development of effective FCC functions. It will also come from financial institutions who have the foresight to drive cultural change by giving strong FCC leaders the platform to successfully push this agenda.

One area where Financial Crime Compliance teams have been pro-active in consistently setting standards globally is in the field of diversity, particularly from a gender perspective. There is still some way to go to truly achieve full diversity, but it's been a proven tool in helping to expand thoughts and challenge normal conventions to push the fight against financial crime forward. In London, we have seen that there are now more female MLRO's than male, and here in the U.S., we're starting to see a similar trend moving forward, with nearly 25% of the CCO's for Foreign Banks here in NYC being female. This is quite a stark contrast to a lot of other senior C-Suite roles."

JEROME MICHAILIDIS: "Certainly. At seminars, we talk a lot about the 'net approach' and challenge if we are doing the best job by simply trying to capture scenarios in filters. One could argue that a more proactive or innovative approach is better, but it's hard to say for sure, because there is a cost in testing new ways of working."

PAUL (PADDY) O'HARA: "PPPs and moving away from tick box financial crime compliance. Getting the frontline (business) to fully embrace FCC risk management."

ANTHONY QUINN: "Absolutely, financial crime costs the global economy over USD$1.45 trillion dollars each year and less than 1% of criminal proceeds are ever recovered – we have a very long way to go on so many fronts.

Firstly, more can be done in enterprise-wide financial crime risk assessments, leveraging proven methodologies, providing industry benchmarks, and generally lifting the capabilities across the market through the adoption of RegTech solutions, which is what we are focused on for our clients at Arctic Intelligence.

Secondly, regulators can be doing more to support the adoption of RegTech solutions to raise the level of acceptance. We still see multi-billion banks and the professional services that support them conducting complex enterprise-wide ML/TF risk assessments using spreadsheets which is clearly not effective.

Thirdly, politicians and regulators need to reduce the attractiveness of organized criminal networks to unregulated sectors. Australia is just about the last country in the world to expand AML/CTF laws to gatekeepers, such as lawyers, accountants, real estate, trust, and company services sectors, and high-value dealers making Australia an attractive country to launder illicit proceeds of crime.

Finally, we are seeing many long-festering issues remaining undetected (and unpunished) for years on end, which indicates that much stronger emphasis needs to be placed on the existence and frequency of independent reviews of financial crime compliance programs to assess the design and operational effectiveness of systems, procedures, and controls in reducing the overall ML/TF risk exposures.

Many organizations do not do a good enough job in this area, and it shows, resulting in costly and distracting remediation programs and financial crime compliance transformation programs which just about every major regulated entity in Australia is undergoing."

JASON HOLT: "Yes, everything I have seen in recent years indicates we need to promote greater partnerships between all the relevant stakeholders in the fight against financial crime. A particularly successful example of such a partnership being the UK JMLIT.

We need far better metrics and a commonly agreed vision of what success looks like in the fight against financial crime.

We need agreement on these across all the relevant stakeholder groups, including Govts, Regulators, Data Protection Authorities, Law Enforcement, FIUs, Shareholders, Financial Institutions and Customers."

MAGGIE QIU: "Certainly! I believe we can do more to utilize data and Technology to detect financial crime patterns and linkages and be faster and more effective."

SCOTT BURTON: "Yes, the FinCEN files amplify this. There is a need for greater public/private information sharing (including the ability to share more freely between market peers). Regulations could consider an enhanced risk-based approach.

Technology needs to be increasingly adopted and partnered with a risk-based approach, which could reduce human error and allow more time for staff to focus on risk management. Developing focused staff training to inexperienced staff is also a key part of financial crime, where we can train and upskill staff into risk managers and educate the front line to recognize red flags."

DEBORAH YOUNG: "If we think of fighting financial crime in simple and personal terms, it's about your parents, your siblings, your children, and your grandmother's right to trust. Trust when interacting and transacting with their financial services provider, their energy company, or their Telco, among others. They deserve trust and know that their provider is operating with the highest standards for advice, products, and data without harming the environment and its people. BUT people in the street do not need to know what RegTech is; it should just be implicit in the trust that they deserve to receive.

Accelerating the adoption of smart technology can counter crimes such as money laundering, CTF, and human trafficking, ensuring we keep the bad actors out. This adoption protects the larger community and will ultimately lower the cost of compliance, make organizations more efficient, reduce the potential of regulatory fines for breaches and build stronger and more robust businesses.

To accelerate adoption, we must have unison across regulators, regulated entities, Government, and RegTech vendors. We must collaborate for the good of the consumer and their safety."

ANTHONY NAPPI: "Technology, the market, products and services, clients and the bad guys are continuing to evolve, and it is extremely important to stay ahead and adapt to these changes. The ability to continually train and educate staff, to use new technologies (i.e. machine learning, NLP etc.), automate manual processes, enable ongoing and continuous monitoring from client onboarding to transaction monitoring, studying issues that have occurred in other institutions and self-test against them to ensure your controls would have caught the issue, running simulations and war games, improving the quality of data, moving away from manual, paper-based onboarding processes to online technology-driven solutions that allow for instantaneous client validation.

There is always more that can and more importantly should be done to protect the company."

GUILLERMO HORTA: "I don't think so, but I think it is time to make a hard stop in conjunction with regulators and legislators, so as an industry, we can make a full assessment around our overall financial crime strategy. In other words, we need to question ourselves if we are truly aiming toward the right things?

Question 5: "Do you believe there is more that we can do to fight financial crime? If so, what more?"

77

Do we have clear and common priorities in our financial crime-fighting agendas at a local and global level? Those are the questions to be raised.

I am convinced that a true risk-based approach should demand a critical focus on those elements of our Financial Crime Program that truly help us identifying and reporting illicit proceeds, rather than those elements that have become just a formal regulatory component providing minimal or no added value against this global phenomenon."

MEL GEORGIE B. RACELA: "Yes. As the AML/CTF supervisor and regulator, the AMLC is aware that it always needs to be one step ahead of money launderers and terrorist financiers to stem their illicit and destructive activities. Perpetrators of financial crime are constantly looking for better, more efficient ways and jurisdictions to launder money or finance terrorism. Given these covered persons, as the first line of defense against money laundering and terrorism financing because they are the ones that deal with potential launderers and financiers, should take the necessary controls and procedures. The AMLC, on the other hand, constantly strives to be ahead of the curve by regularly conducting supervision, compliance-checking, and capacity building activities to ensure that covered persons (such as financial institutions and other entities covered under the AMLA, as amended) comply with the requirements of the AMLA, as amended, and its Implementing Rules and Regulations on customer identification, recordkeeping, and reporting of covered and suspicious transactions.

But rather than just acting as a regulator all the time, we initiated a partnership program called the Public-Private Partnership Program (PPPP). The PPPP allows the AMLC and the private sector to work within a framework that encourages coordination and collaboration in the areas of information exchange and capacity-building to enhance each other's abilities to address money laundering, terrorism, and terrorism financing concerns. It is an alternative to the rigid, rule-based approach to compliance with the law. The government presents itself as an authority, ensuring compliance under the consequence of penalties and sanctions. Through the PPPP, both parties enter into a partnership to institutionalize an effective documentation mechanism that performs targeted suspicious transaction monitoring and reporting; and develops valuable or breakthrough investigative leads.

For instance, the AMLC shared its first study on child pornography (covering the period 2015 to 2018), which includes the list of approximately 3,000 POIs with its PPPP partners. These partners, in turn, incorporated the findings of the study and the names of the identified suspected offenders and facilitators in their respective AML/CTF monitoring systems. This then disrupted payments before transfers related to OSEC. This partnership provides valuable intelligence and alerts on financial transactions relative to OSEC that pass through the private sectors' platforms and clients who avail of their services. As a result, suspicious transaction reporting on OSEC increased by more than 11,000%. Moreover, upon updating the study to cover the period 2019 until the first half of 2020, the POIs increased more than sevenfold."

MARTA LIA REQUEIJO: "The current anti-money laundering regime is not effective. Two main challenges must be addressed: cross-border flows and asymmetry of information.

Financial flows are exchanged between several entities in a cross-border way. Therefore, to be successful, we need to have a joint and global approach in preventing and detecting financial crime activity. A more effective strategic response would be based on:

- Information sharing cross-border.

- An investigation-led approach driven by public and private sector partnerships such as the Joint Money Laundering Intelligence Taskforce, in the U.K."

CARLOS GARCIA PAVIA: "Data is undoubtedly the most essential asset to effectively combat financial crime. Unfortunately, poor quality data is a common denominator across many financial institutions. For some, customer records are not current, are incomplete, or are inaccurate. Hence, tampering with the effectiveness of the overall FCC controls.

There is a need for financial institutions to devote funding and effort to remediate the data in their systems of record to enhance the quality of the data flowing through their FCC processes. This requires the commitment from lines of business and Chief Data Officers to raise the bar on the definition of sound data quality standards, data management policies, and proper data governance.

The data collection channels need to be enhanced to ensure all data elements are properly captured and digitized from origination. Personnel involved in data collection need to be better trained on properly capturing complete and accurate data. Perhaps one of the most common problems in the industry is the use of non-standard abbreviations to try to fit data into fields with limited length. I have seen some cases where it is virtually impossible to make sense of some of the abbreviations used in some jurisdictions.

There is also a need for financial institutions to be able to integrate a full view of their customer's footprint within their organization. The risk associated with customers having multiple relationships across lines of business or multiple jurisdictions may seem quite different when not considering a fully integrated view of all those relationships. Financial institutions need to be able to connect the dots not only between those multiple relationships but also to understand the associated parties that may be in the mix.

More transparent and close collaboration amongst financial institutions is also prime to strengthen the fight against financial crime."

REFLECTION

How can you apply these lessons and insights to your career or life today?

_____

_____

_____

_____

_____

_____

_____

_____

_____

_____

_____

_____

What would you change
about financial crime risk and
compliance programs?

QUESTION 6

TADEO (JUN) CLARAVALL: "There are many, but my effort and attention presently are in two areas of the financial crime risk and compliance program, which I think needs a major overhaul; Financial Crimes Training and Financial Crimes Metrics.

Traditional Financial Crime training methods, specifically online, one-way lectures, using 'textbook' style teaching have limited effectiveness. Learners remember information only long enough to pass the test at the end, then most of what's learned is not retained nor applied in their work. As a result, learners are mostly disinterested and go through the motions to complete an online financial crime course for the sake of compliance. By missing out on effective financial crime learning, learners cannot skill-up, which affects their ability to ultimately make sound business and risk management decisions regarding financial crimes.

The change I'm seeking to make is to move towards doing workshops that are learner-centered, self-paced, project-based, and peer-supported.

Next, the current conventional approach to metrics measures financial crime risk and operational effectiveness using compliance-focused data points. What's lacking is that current metrics don't adequately measure effectiveness from the perspective of actual risk mitigation events, such as identifying and reporting possible criminal activity and interdicting criminal proceeds. In addition, business metrics in the form of financial cost of controls and cost of potential regulatory penalties are also not adequately measured and reported. Furthermore, current business and risk reporting is cumbersome to prepare, voluminous and wordy in content, and not reader-friendly.

The change I'm seeking to make is a move towards more data visualization of the right metrics in a format that is easy to prepare and easy to read will result in better monitoring of financial crime risks, threats, and costs, thereby assisting in better business and risk decision making."

NICK TURNER: "Companies should have a clear understanding of their roles and responsibilities. In the big picture, a bank is not a law

Question 6: "What would you change about financial
crime risk and compliance programs?"

83

enforcement agency. Its role is to follow the rules that apply to it and to refer suspicious activity or violations of law to the proper authorities.

Similarly, companies are not responsible for their counterparties' compliance, although they should certainly discourage non-compliance.

The cost of not getting this balance right is that our customers and counterparties have expectations placed on them that go above and beyond what the law requires."

JOHN FOGARTY: "Risk-based programs are sometimes the hardest to implement, and as the world changes and develops, the way we think about the financial crime should also. Most programs in place within banking institutions follow the same tried and tested path that has been in place for the best part of the past 15 years. This manual approach with static data is being replaced with automated technology advancements allowing for dynamic real-time risk assessments and network analysis. The sooner organizations can move to this model, the better programs will become – however, it's critical that the Data is accurate and complete before you flick the switch!"

JAIKUMAR (JAI) RAMASWAMY: "The most difficult aspect of creating a financial crimes compliance program is balancing the need for processes and controls that implement financial crimes policies in a large and complex organization with the imperative of identifying illicit financial activity.

Auditors and regulatory examiners/supervisors tend to approach financial crimes compliance in the same way that they approach other types of risk management, focusing on controls and testing. But financial crimes compliance involves more than just creating auditable processes. — it should be focused on preventing and detecting actually illicit activity. Compliance professionals will always respond to audit and examination findings because these are the immediate sources of pain that they experience — however this tends to result in layers of "checkers checking checkers" that reduces audit findings but does not lead to the catching illicit activity.

Since illicit financial activity is a small portion of what happens in a financial institution, this type of check the box exercise ends up in a disproportionate amount of time spent ensuring the collection of information on likely innocent parties rather than focusing resources on higher-risk activity. As a result, while AML regimes nominally follow a risk-based approach, they are in practice closer to zero tolerance regimes.

Taking the risk-based approach seriously would involve re-allocating resources from low-value activities to activities actually designed to find the needle in the haystack. This might require accepting higher rates of operational failure for these low-risk activities, but would result in more bad guys being caught."

MARTIN JAMES WALLIS: "I think the programs are already moving in the right direction with the use of technology to provide greater accuracy and clarity of information. This means that analysts can make better well-informed judgments on what suspicious activity is. Ensuring these are integrated, adaptable, and easy to understand is vital if we want these to be used to impact and not overcomplicate or overburden the teams that would rely on them. The ability for these systems to learn and develop does need to be monitored not to introduce bias or make judgments all by themselves; context is important. Many in the FinTech and RegTech space have some great systems that are constantly evolving and are working at achieving that delicate balance. Unfortunately, there is no one size fits all solution.

However, behind any of these solutions is the human element, and we should not think that technology can replace all of this. Improving diversity within the people that support these programs enables broader perspectives, allowing for more inclusive systems and controls. This includes the protected categories and areas such as social mobility. Wider teams reduce the capacity for groupthink, minimize bias, and provide better understanding and insight across the board, whether in project delivery, management, setting or testing systems, or getting into the weeds of an investigation. There are multiple benefits to be gained from embracing a more diverse workforce, and this should be encouraged and nurtured at every level. It should not be seen as a separate sidebar activity but embedded as part of the fabric of an organization."

JEROME MICHAILIDIS: "I would like to simplify them. I think if they become too complex, then the Business cannot adequately implement them."

PATRICIA SULLIVAN: "While I fully support the objective of 'fighting financial crime' in FCC programs, I think there needs to be more

Question 6: "What would you change about financial crime risk and compliance programs?"

85

focus on the role strong FCC programs can have in promoting financial inclusion and sustainable outcomes in our communities. I would like to see a greater convergence of the ESG agenda and FCC in banks (and on the public side) and how teams and programs are structured. Through my work at Lawyers Without Borders, this convergence is very clear. For example, by supporting effective governance and the rule of law in countries, there is a corresponding benefit in reducing the predicate offenses that underpin money laundering."

DEBORAH YOUNG: "Empower and equip the risk managers within regulated entities with the best and most contemporary tools that can surface, manage and report financial crime risks earlier with more transparency and in real-time. They exist; they just need to be adopted sooner. Boards and leadership teams must understand as a given what RegTech is and what it can achieve for them. We must drive change around digital transformation programs to include consideration of the traditional blockers for innovative technology solutions including I.T. security and procurement processes."

ABTAR RANDHAWA: "I would implement reviews such as control reviews, thematic reviews, and regulatory lines of business reviews. With the added component of performing live and hot reviews. The benefits of this include a point in time opinion and views of regulatory compliance, the effectiveness of change management, changes in the control environment and any other capability of financial crime environment."

ANTHONY QUINN: "For a long time, regulated entities have failed to take their AML/CTF obligations seriously and, there has been a lack of consequences on employees or directors for ineffective financial crime compliance programs.

All too often, when things go wrong it's the shareholders that bear the impact with falling share prices, canceled dividends, costly fines, and remediation/transformation programs going on for years and years, so I would like to see the increase in personal civil and criminal liability on Directors and employees, in the cases of willful blindness, negligence, incompetence or all three."

YVETTE CHEAK: "Each bank has its own Compliance Program. What is important is not to just understand the law but to understand the business of the institution. Know the risks and type of controls needed. Have a strong KYC due diligence program, monitoring transactions, and scrutiny of transactions for alert management to prevent the firm from being used for illegal facilitations."

ROD FRANCIS: "Ohh, where do I start! Firstly, let's stop talking about 'programs'! Let's think and discuss risk! Often the discussions I have had within FI's drag me to focus on elements of the program and not around underlying risk. We can often clearly articulate how our program operates. Still, we can't articulate how it effectively and efficiently (not a dirty word) manages or mitigates the risk (to an acceptable level – difficult to eliminate – leads to risk appetite). I think that has and continues to be missing. We end up managing regulatory risk or internal stakeholder's vs. financial crime compliance risk. I'm being unfair as I feel the industry/discussion has changed/moved forward, but every FCC officer should help their organization change the narrative. We need to talk about risk! We all need to take responsibility for that risk.

If you can't really articulate the underlying risk and why your policy, your standard is written in a way that mitigates that risk. Or why a regulator actually defines a rule in a certain way to actually mitigate the risk. If you think there are other ways to mitigate that risk and have been too restricted, that's kind of a separate conversation that I think has its consequences.

Your stakeholders can sometimes be annoying, but they are very intelligent people, and they will be banging on what we are really trying to achieve here. And if you can at least articulate, they may not agree with you. But if you can't articulate it, that's a real problem, and that's why often you get financial institutions that have good programs that on paper look okay, that are pretty strong. But when you scratch the surface, they don't really address the risk and the journey not implemented."

ERIC FAVILA: "The composition of talent in the sector. Currently, it is heavy on the legal and risk management profession. It is still a profession without a natural progression from the formal education system. It makes sense to draw lawyers and risk managers because they can interpret regulations and understand the business of finance. FC Professionals tend to accidentally stumble into this career. Recently we see more and more former law enforcement, former regulators, and technologists pursue careers in financial crime prevention. And this is exciting. What I would like to see more in the space are gamers. Yes, gamers, and why not? Preventing

Question 6: "What would you change about financial crime risk and compliance programs?"

87

financial crime is about strategy, solving complex puzzles, and creative thinking. It is not simply about compliance with the rules. Especially with principles-based regulation, there is a channel for innovative thinkers to engage regulators, question the rule book, help improve it and develop effective and sustainable solutions. By this, it means solutions strike a balance between commercial interests and the spirit of the law. Nefarious elements are essentially gaming the system. So why not have an opposing force of gamers ensuring the safety of the financial system?

It is hard to imagine university students aspiring to be compliance officers coming out of school. I'm not even sure aspiring lawyers consider that as the first port of call. Not even a financial crime fighter. Why? I think it is because it's unclear what a financial crime fighter is. Though it is nice to see references of financial crime fighters in TV and movies they're mainly in the background and play a supporting role in the bigger picture. To the unfamiliar, it sounds like a miserable back-office bank job. People still aspire to be in law enforcement, finance, engineering, the arts, and many others because they resonate with purpose. Financial crime risk and compliance have been around long enough and it is high time that it develops into a career to aspire to rather than stumble upon. It is not simply about following the rules set by the regulators. I see it as a critical element in ensuring the safety of the financial system and protecting the vulnerable."

MEL GEORGIE B. RACELA: "Continuity and consistency. The aspects of AML/CTF transform continuously to reach optimization to meet regulatory requirements and respond to the evolving financial crime techniques and mitigate the impact of associated risks while sustaining the operational efficiency of the business. A person involved in financial crime must continuously educate to evolve alongside the modus operandi of criminals.

For the AMLC, we do not have any issue with continuity because the Executive Director has a five-year term. But for the other LEAs, especially the PNP, their Chief constantly changes. With the change in the leadership comes replacements in key positions within its organization. When that happens, we start all over again to educate, collaborate, and commit. We do not mind doing this, as we are used to this system, but we waste precious time doing this. LEAs must therefore have a financial program that is well disseminated to potential leaders so that it may continuously and consistently be implemented regardless of the new leader's thrust.

The same principle applies to compliance programs. The intricacy of financial crimes and the decentralized approach in detection and prevention call for diverse skills and broad-based knowledge across the financial crime spectrum. Moreover, financial crimes are often undertaken with complexity that they demand, at least, equally sophisticated detection and prevention measures. With this said, compliance initiatives must start from the top, the Chairperson of the BOD or the BOD itself. This ensures continuity and consistency, especially when a compliance program is looked upon as an investment in the company's reputation rather than a cost of doing business. When culture starts from the top, policies and resources become responsive and effective."

JESSICA HODSON: "The rush to move into AI and technology. It is always the FinTech's who want to move from excel spreadsheets, straight to a 2050 futuristic system. I think more emphasis should be placed on laying the foundations of data and M.I before firms start looking for the quickest ways to capture or find trends.

Basically, walk before you can run!"

PAUL (PADDY) O'HARA: "PPPs and moving away from tick box financial crime compliance. Getting the frontline (business) to fully embrace FCC risk management."

ANTHONY NAPPI: "Four areas:

Further alignment and integration between the businesses and functions with the second and third lines of defense leads to a better understanding of the control requirements as well as taking greater responsibility and ownership of the execution, implementation and ongoing refinement of the control environment.

Simplify, streamline, and reduce the procedures and processes – I can remember that there were hundreds of changes to the AML program in 12 months – this is way too much for any organization to digest, understand and execute against. The most damaging impact is that you lose the organization as it feels that they will never be able to understand or implement this magnitude of changes and simply give up!

Automation of testing that the controls are fit for purpose and are working as designed and that the regulations are fully aligned to each control.

Question 6: "What would you change about financial crime risk and compliance programs?"

89

The ability to share data and information with other Financial Services companies so that the "bad actors" simply do not move from one bank to another – also getting information back from SARs that are filed so as to understand the use cases – and how to build better products, better testing, better controls, to be able to blacklist companies and individuals."

GUILLERMO HORTA: "I would make emphasis on the use of AI, data analytics and other new technologies that can give you a better view of what is truly suspicious, rather than using linear transaction monitoring systems that have a very low conversation ratio between alerts and SARs.

I would also promote the use of government-funded programs to thoroughly identify individuals and companies on a national or even global scale, facilitating financial inclusion and making it easier for Banks to complete KYC and EDD processes. As an example, millions of travellers use today the Global Entry and Trusted Traveller Programs, which facilitate the identification of US and foreign individuals at entry ports into the US. If a similar program would exist at a KYC level, you could potentially be able to provide your "Trusted Bank Client" identification number without any additional hassle from a KYC perspective."

How can you apply these lessons and insights to your career or life today?

_____

_____

_____

_____

_____

_____

_____

_____

_____

_____

_____

_____

_____

What is the role of technology in your current job?
Do you think it will be more critical with the threat of COVID-19?

QUESTION 7

TADEO (JUN) CLARAVALL: "Technology is a tool that I use to be more effective at my work. When I started in financial crime two decades ago, we had computers but with comparatively weak computing power. We also had very little software, mainly M.S. Office applications. Today, the hardware and software I use are exponentially better and more powerful, thereby optimizing my work productivity.

I believe that in the next decade, tech innovations with wearables, cloud, blockchain, and A.I. will radically change how we fight financial crimes. Robots and algorithms will take over many of the basic and manual tasks we perform, leaving us to create such robots and algorithms, tuning and maintaining them, and taking action on the outputs.

COVID did not trigger any of these advancements, but it hastened its development and implementation."

ANTHONY QUINN: "I am the founder of a RegTech business called Arctic Intelligence and even prior to COVID, but increasingly with more people working from remote locations, being able to collaborate in an effective way using cloud-based technology solutions is increasingly becoming critical for regulated entities to consider the adoption of financial crime RegTech solutions."

JEROME MICHAILIDIS: "It is mostly to provide tools and solutions for industrialization. For some, it is probably also robotics and AI, but I don't see that as much. I think the biggest change from Covid is that we have to be more reliant on IT support for things such as continuity measures and ongoing digital support."

JOHN CUSACK: "Technology remains a crucial enabler to fighting financial crime along with people, process and data. The combination of these 4 elements can strengthen programmes as well as make them more efficient. There are a plethora of new technologies now available that offer solutions that are really interesting. I'd pick a couple, for example technology that can help to better profile customers their transactions and

Question 7: "What is the role of technology in your current job?
Do you think it will be more critical with the threat of COVID-19?"

93

connections so that a more rounded view can be taken. Entity resolution technology helps firms identify connections that traditional approaches miss and consequently optimise the KYC and TM process and significantly aid financial crime investigators. Another area is using machine learning to understand how expert hit handling is carried out and in so doing generate a cohort of machine experts that can transparently outperform many average or even seasoned analysts. Lastly by reimagining how things are done today we can solve problems in new and interesting ways. Why for example is sanctions screening performed the way it is when there are much better alternatives that should be explored. For example why not imagine a collective effort, embracing technologies that can enhance watchlists, screen transactions generate high quality alerts and disposition many of these based on machine learning, entity resolution and information exchange. A real game changer, increasing effectiveness, improving efficiency and reducing unwanted friction and enhancing the customer experience. Even here whilst technology plays a role it is the combination of people process technology and data that will bring the best results."

ERIC FAVILA: "My job is predominantly advisory in nature helping financial institutions design and implement effective and sustainable financial crime prevention programs. It is through this work that I appreciate the critical role technology plays in combatting financial crime. Covering the range of vulnerabilities, breadth of data points, and speed at which criminal elements adapt can only be done sustainably and effectively with technology. That said, it is important to consider that the foundations of the program (policies, procedures, roles & responsibilities, etc) are robust and thoughtfully designed. It strikes a balance between three pillars:1) obligations (regulatory and institutional risk appetite), 2) operational impact and 3) client experience. Neglecting any pillar guarantees problems down the road. Applying technology to an inadequately designed program only aggravates the problem. What do you get when you automate a bad process? A really fast but bad process.

In the COVID-19 pandemic, we have seen a material shift to digital payments and platforms. This is where technology has home-court advantage. Monitoring electronic payments are simpler compared to tracking cash movements. Tough typologies may change, there are new technologies that are able to detect anomalies to signal experts to assess emerging risks.

One area of my work is in advising financial institutions, regulators, law enforcement, and advocacy groups in the Philippines on combatting the Online Sexual Exploitation of Children (OSEC) through payment interdiction. Before the pandemic, there was a split between online and in-person abuse. In-person abuse entails cash. During the pandemic, the crime has moved almost exclusively online giving the opportunity for the financial services sector to play an active role in combating OSEC. There has been a lot of attention drawn to the role of social media companies and internet service providers to detect and report OSEC. As with all financial crimes, OSEC is commercially driven. Unlike most financial crimes, however, payments related to OSEC are not proceeds of the crime but rather the facilitation of. Detection is closer to detecting terrorist financing and fraud rather than money laundering."

MARTIN JAMES WALLIS: "From an internal perspective, the use of data and automation are key for FINTRAIL as with many companies. Automation allows us to maximize the impact of the teams' efforts, allowing them to focus on their core focus of fighting financial crime rather than getting bogged down with some of the repetitive and manual administrative tasks. These also help in the delivery of our services by improving collaboration. There are some great systems out there, and with a lot of the non-code platforms, it means that most can immediately gain benefit. Collecting and analyzing data in a meaningful way is also important, whether that is employee satisfaction, project management, or forecasting future resource requirements. We all live in data-rich environments that can enable our work, but we need to be clear from the outset and transparent about what is being collected and how it is being used.

When working with FinTech and RegTech, there is no doubt that technology is fundamental to their offerings. From our experience at FINTRAIL, working with top companies in the sector means we have been able to learn how best to support integration, calibration, assurance testing and tuning, and due diligence so that our clients can feel confident that their systems are performing as required and fulfilling their regulatory, operational, technical, and commercial needs. Many would agree that COVID-19 has accelerated digital transformation globally, not only in the financial sector. Many organizations were thinking about moving to a more digital approach; for some, it has been a period of massive growth, e.g., Zoom. However, where we see benefits from globalization and the removal of geographic barriers, criminals can operate globally and ob-

Question 7: "What is the role of technology in your current job? Do you think it will be more critical with the threat of COVID-19?"

95

fuscate their activity through what can sometimes be complex networks. Technology can help to identify and track some of this activity. However, I think it will still need a keen and analytical mind to consider what is being delivered and make it actionable, at least for now!

Another key aspect is the future of work and that now remote working has become the norm; what will a post-COVID-19 world look like. We had already embraced flexible working, but the pandemic has shown us that remote working can be a viable option, and this is now forming part of our future operating model. Remaining connected as an organization keeping those touchpoints that enable and maintain relationships is something that has been missing in the fully remote world, and it is something we will include in our working environment while still keeping the flexibility of WFH."

YVETTE CHEAK: "I am an honorary adviser and work mainly in an advisory capacity. However, I do have a role of the need and use of technology, which is critical to monitor transactions, but what is more important are the parameters used to discover alerts. Nothing should replace experienced personnel to detect what is a true alert from a false positive."

MARLENE MELI: "Working for a software company that provides financial crime mitigation solutions, technology plays a key role. Especially with the latest developments in artificial intelligence (A.I.) and their promises for much better detection of true alerts without the noise of false positives. However, the latest technologies do not improve efficiency and detection rates when there is a lack of skilled staff to properly calibrate and configure the systems.

One of my workmates used the analogy of cooking in this regard: you can have all the ingredients you need and use the kitchen equipment of a Gault-Millau restaurant, but when you lack the skills to cook like a Chef, you will never succeed in making the best out of ingredients and equipment. And this is very true in fighting financial crime as well. Technology is an enabler, but the skilled staff is the key to make the best out of the latest technology.

Yes, I think that technology becomes even more critical these days due to COVID-19. We have seen a sharp increase in fraud cases, and more people are exposed to fraud attempts since a forced home office in a large number of countries. As a consequence, firms, online shops, and banks face an increasing number of fraudulent transactions and payments. Those applying A.I. to detect suspicious transactions might be challenged to more frequently update their risk models in order to cope with the increase of fraud attempts."

MATT FRIEDMAN: "The Mekong Club's Modern Slavery Risk Map is a technology tool that amalgamates key data sources related to global modern slavery risk into one central location, allowing banks to filter and search by country to view the most up-to-date figures on modern slavery risk taken from publicly available sources. This tool is often incorporated into risk assessment processes in order to assess client risk ratings in the bank. The following data sources are included in this tool:

- Global Slavery Index: Provides a country by country ranking of the number of people in modern slavery, as well as an analysis of the actions that governments are taking to respond, and the factors that make people vulnerable.

- US State Department's Trafficking in Person's Report: This report is produced on an annual basis by the US State Department and ranks country responses to modern slavery on a tiered basis. The report also includes narrative and recommendations on the trafficking situation in each country globally.

- Department of Labor's List of Goods Produced by Child Labor or Forced Labor: This annual publication is issued by the United States Government's Bureau of International Labor Affairs at the U.S. Department of Labor. It provides a list of known commodities and goods that have forced and child labor issues as well as details on the locations where the risk is highest.

- Verité Commodity Atlas: This resource, maintained by Verite, helps explore and understand the connection between specific commodities and forced labor (and other forms of exploitation). It continues to be updated regularly with all 43 commodities from the report.

We anticipate that this kind of tool to track and analyze data will be more critical as the COVID-19 crisis continues to unfold. With more people entering into indebtedness situations, the vulnerability of modern slavery has gone up significantly."

Question 7: "What is the role of technology in your current job?
Do you think it will be more critical with the threat of COVID-19?"

97

ROD FRANCIS: "Technology is at the top of the list. As a consultant, it's on the agenda of most of my clients. The better use of data and technology to drive their risk management programs has been critical as we move forward. Technology is essential to our current COVID-19 world. Still, I would argue it is critical from a business perspective and how FI's deliver their products and services to clients in a very different world. Risk management (including FCC) must follow the same path; otherwise, STP delivery and a great client experience will be compromised.

Regulators must support technology change and provide some space for FI's to be innovative. There is a lot of talk and theory, but there are still significant regulatory barriers speaking to FI's. Why are we still undertaking traditional rules-based transaction-based monitoring? We need 'digital' solutions for a digital world, not maintaining 'analog solutions.

I do appreciate the challenges that regulators face. However, the need to be brave and allow and support a pivot to better data and technology-driven risk management methods is critical. This is in an environment where our markets have and continue to change rapidly with new risks entering the ecosystem."

GUILLERMO HORTA: "Absolutely. As a Financial Crime professional involved in these topics for more than 20 years, I considered that the key elements of an AML or Financial Crime Programs are the technological capabilities that you can have to monitor and detect suspicious activity. Covid-19 has moved millions of people from traditional ways of Banking to online and remote Banking platforms. Generation Z is clearly dependant on technology, and I personally can't imagine my 12-year-old daughter walking into a branch in 8 years to make a check deposit.

Banking as we know it will need to adapt and evolve quickly to serve the demand of a technology-based generation demanding real-time payments and global capabilities."

JOHN FOGARTY: "I am running a large FCC remediation program at the moment, which is essentially a large technology program. Underpinning any AML program at its core is good technology infrastructure - onboarding systems, customer risk assessments, transaction monitoring and sanction screening systems, investigative case management tools with overarching network analysis. Each with the ability to interact with one another using complete and accurate customer and payment data. Technology advancements are always critical in the fight against financial crime, trying to keep pace with criminal networks. COVID-19, if anything, evidenced that we don't need face-to-face interactions, and a program can operate electronically – including Identification verification through forms of biometrics. Embedding this technology into everything we do is now the challenge."

ABTAR RANDHAWA: "Technology is the critical golden source of everything we do. Our systems are our processes and allow us to connect procedures to processes. Sadly, Technology has become very complex, and updating and changing the underlying purposes of a system is extremely challenging as the impact any change has could hold huge ramifications for the client, regulatory adherence, and evolving a solution into an 'unknown' area. All of this requires the appropriate level of program management skills, sophisticated change management tools, and acceptable levels of UAT and parallel runs to ensure the solution provides the expected outcome. Management and especially technology leaders combining integrated risk management with an enterprise view of risk across lines of business and value chains will help align the overall risk management strategy further. Technology has a key part to play in shaping risk appetite as controls and processes built within our systems enable us to have confidence in the robustness of our control environment."

JASON HOLT: "Technology sits at the very core of Exiger's consulting business, which revolves around our proprietary technology that uses AI, Machine learning, Natural language processing, and many other forms of innovative technology to help firms better manage their financial crimes risks.

COVID-19 has accelerated the use of technology at many firms. In particular, it acted as a catalyst for some to go live with AI technology, for example, to close out transaction monitoring alerts (as inventories of alerts aged, while investigators struggled to get online and access all the internal tools they required). With firms coming to terms with remote working, they have also become more willing to share data with third parties and to allow them to work remotely also."

NICK TURNER: "As much as I miss traveling the globe, I've learned that a lot of what I do can be done just as well over video conference.

I can meet with way more clients in a day now than when I had to spend time traveling to their locations!"

Question 7: "What is the role of technology in your current job? Do you think it will be more critical with the threat of COVID-19?"

99

DEBORAH YOUNG: "I commenced my career in financial services 30 years ago when hardcover ledgers were the risk management tool of the day.

Fast forward to today, we are using technology in all parts of our daily life. About five years ago, I was interested in how technology was changing the face of financial services as an enabler.

As the founding CEO of The RegTech Association, I've learned. I now advocate for technology to be adopted that brings trust at scale, enables organizations to make better business decisions, helps keep citizens safe, and underpins a solid regulatory system and economy.

The RegTech Association has 180 organizations as members who are part of our global center for RegTech excellence. Of those, 130 are RegTech companies that are solving the greatest regulation and compliance challenges, and 25% or almost a quarter of these are helping organizations fight financial crime.

The pandemic has heightened the need for great RegTech as the volume of data flowing around the system has increased; the need to preserve privacy and security has been elevated, workers have pivoted to a hybrid or working from a home model that has called for organizations to by hyper-vigilant about where and what exposures their business or customer information has."

MEL GEORGIE B. RACELA: "Being a regulator, the AMLC's initiatives are mainly geared toward supervisory technology solutions, even before the Covid-19 pandemic. To make sense of big data received from covered persons, the AMLC maintains a semi-automated in-house profiling system for STRs and a proprietary data-mining tool, using covered transaction report data to automate the flagging of subjects with unusual transaction activity and patterns. The AMLC likewise procures subscriptions to proprietary screening platforms and secure electronic access to domestic government agency databases to expand the scope of its intelligence-gathering.

Further, aligned with the growing importance of financial and regulatory technology in shaping the financial landscape, in 2018, the AMLC released the Guidelines on the Digitization of Customer Records in 2018 and a study that analyzed the profile of transactions passing through Philippine-regulated virtual asset service providers (VASPs). The AMLC also continually engages with technology-driven sectors, such as remittance and payments services companies, to augment its intelligence-gathering. Likewise, the AMLC participates in multilateral projects with other FIUs to contribute to and learn from the global and regional discourse on emerging technologies.

As firms and consumers alike have been compelled to tap into technological solutions to adjust to the new economy of physical distancing, electronic payments, and decreased manpower, the pandemic may have buoyed demand for regulatory and financial technology solutions. There will be more profound changes as the quarantine measures has forced the AMLC, supervising authorities, and covered persons to quickly adapt to work disruptions by employing the latest technology, skeleton workforce, and work-from-home arrangements.

In 2020, the AMLC conducted the study, "COVID-19 Financial Crime Trend Analysis and Typologies Brief, Series 1 and 2." For the guidance of government and law enforcement agencies, covered persons, and the public, this is AMLC's initiative of analyzing financial crime trends in the Philippines, covering a period of the pandemic, and using STRs filed by covered persons.

Based on the study, 49% of the STRs are related to skimming, phishing, unauthorized transactions, and other violations of the Electronic Commerce Act with an estimated value of PhP2.7 billion. Moreover, the volume of e-money-related STRS has grown faster than cash-related STRs. From 2017 to 2020, e-money-related STRs increased by 988%, while cash- and check-related STRs grew only by 47%.

Clearly, criminals have been leveraging on technology. The ease of online retail fund transfers, not to mention the accelerated adoption of digital processes by many institutions brought about by the pandemic, may have altered the flow of funds from cash to digital transactions.

Technology works both ways: It can help facilitate crimes that have been worsened by the adverse economic effects of the pandemic. But technology, along with heightened awareness among stakeholders, can also prevent crime.

Institutions should learn lessons from studies, such as the AMLC's Covid-19 study, and strive to become more agile and prepared for any eventuality due to the pandemic or its result. They should leverage cybersecurity as the pandemic has seen a surge in electronic payments and attendant cyber-related crimes. Automation, through artificial intelligence and digitization projects, may be prioritized to continue the progress made during the pandemic. Before embarking on such ambitious projects, however, financial institutions must recognize that the skills of their specialists are aligned with their investments and that they should consider capacity building as the top priority."

MAGGIE QIU: "Technology is a critical tool in my current job to identify relationships and transactions with sanctioned countries and parties. I think with the threat of COVID-19, this tool is becoming more and more important, and it will be more accurate, more efficient, and ultimately bring true efficiencies into fighting financial crimes."

CARLOS GARCIA PAVIA: "The use of technology is becoming even more important every day as data is exponentially increasing at an accelerated pace as the use of digital financial services is expanding. As a result, the size and complexity of the data lakes in all financial institutions are increasing rapidly.

Events like the recent COVID-19 pandemic trigger a sudden transformation of the way customers and financial institutions interact around the world.

Making sense of a massive amount of new information within a minimum amount of time is essential to keep financial services going without compromising the effectiveness and efficiency of the FCC programs.

The use of analytics to extract actionable intelligence to effectively manage and mitigate financial crime risk is of the utmost importance. Having timely access to the right data and through the right technology toolset make all the difference in the decision-making process.

Partnership and collaboration across risk owners, control owners, risk stewards, CDO, I.T., and Analytics, is and will continue to be absolutely necessary to ensure the proper use and adoption of emerging technologies to truly resolve current and upcoming challenges. Some of the emerging FinTech/RegTech solutions may be incredibly attractive and promising at first sight, but organizations must truly evaluate the soundness of their design and feasibility to be integrated and deployed within the existing control and governance framework. Running a proof of concept or isolated test of these solutions is quite different from industrializing such solutions to be deployed at a larger scale.

Although the pursuit of innovation is obviously required to keep the lead in the fight against financial crime, we must be very self-aware of avoiding the pursuit of all new and shiny objects on the horizon as only very few of them are worth pursuing. Then, there is the risk of early adoption of emerging technologies; will it work? Will it deliver what is expected? Will, it really brings savings to the organization, or will it only shift the cost from one side to the other?

Some emerging FinTech/RegTech companies seem to offer very clever solutions, in theory and on paper. The reality is that some of these emerging players may have brilliant theoretical ideas yet to be proven in real-life financial services scenarios. Some of them offer their products under the banner of being Minimum Viable Products (MVPs) yet requiring a good deal of further development. Typically, they require the business knowledge and functional expertise of the financial institutions to actually being able to deliver a finished product. In other words, the financial institutions pay a hefty price tag to help these emerging players develop finished products that end up being sold many times over to others.

Organizations seeking innovation using emerging I.T. players must have eyes wide open to identify investment worthy I.T. players which can be incubated to become solid market disruptors. Practicing this principle is an actual win-win for both financial institutions and emerging I.T. players. The financial institution gets the solution it needs, and the emerging player gets investment capital to execute their product and market strategy to grow their business. At the end of the day, this partnership provides a solid and rapid return on investment to the financial institution, converting the development cost into an actual investment with a profitable return. Some financial institutions are already following this principle with a very promising outlook."

PAUL (PADDY) O'HARA: "I think Covid has sped it up. Technology helps with both cutting down false positives, so work can be done on the risk, but also enhancing investigative techniques to find patterns and activity that humans can't find on their own."

JESSICA HODSON: "Technology in recruitment is obviously really important (and no, we don't use "CV scanning tools") and something which we, like every other sector, need to invest and continually improve in.

From a financial crime perspective, it's important I keep up with incoming technology and what the firms are looking to use. For example, in 2021 we have seen a huge wave of financial crime systems special-ists, where firms are looking for in-house resource to better manage these for them, moving away from having external consultants. Understanding what good looks like in this space is important.

The people in these roles know how to read data with a financial crime lens, but more importantly, they know how to explain the findings and make recommendations. This means we are seeing more people who can amend the typologies as well as almost an advisory type role.

COVID-19 has brought about a difference in how businesses contin-gency plan for their financial crime functions and they are turning to technology to help with this. An example we are seeing is a repercussion from the initial lockdown where many banks had large off -shore hubs as part of their contingency plan. When the world shut down, they were left in a vulnerable position as these offices closed.

The reaction to this has to bring a small number of these roles brough back to the UK, or home country away from these cheaper hubs. These roles have aligned with technology to make them more efficient and effec-tive to ensure the higher cost remains of value."

How can you apply these lessons and insights to your career or life today?

_____

_____

_____

_____

_____

_____

_____

_____

_____

_____

_____

_____

_____

_____

If financial crime fighters want to stay relevant in this coming age of A.I. and machine learning technologies, what do you think are the most important steps for them to take?

QUESTION 8

TADEO (JUN) CLARAVALL: "I use the START/ STOP/ MORE/ LESS formula when dealing with any significant change that comes my way. The coming wave of exponential technologies, including A.I., machine learning, and blockchain, will radically change finance as we know it and, by extension, financial crimes.

We need to START learning about these technologies. How do we learn? Learning professionals say that we learn from Experience, Exposure, and Education. As financial crime fighters, we should do all three. Start with educating ourselves about these technologies, what it can do, what it can't do, how it works, how can it be utilized, and how can it be misused. That last point is crucial. With this knowledge, we next must find ways to expose ourselves to these technologies as a consumer. For example, to understand blockchain better, maybe we should invest in cryptocurrencies which is one blockchain application. By doing so, we can experience the end-to-end process ourselves. Nothing beats hands-on experience.

We need to STOP all excuses (e.g. I'm too busy) and limiting beliefs about our ability to understand and get on top of these technologies (e.g. I'm not a techie). Busy is a choice. Saying I'm too busy to take the time and effort to study this important topic is akin to a carpenter saying I'm too busy sawing wood with my old hacksaw to learn to use power saws that do the job in 1/20th of the time and effort. It's a ridiculous excuse. At present, there are so many free and paid resources online to learn these technologies. You don't need to go back to higher learning institutions to get a post-grad degree on this. Examples of what I use personally, aside from reading books written by experts on this subject are, M.I.T. Open-CourseWare (free) and Udemy (paid). Set aside 30 min/day and start learning now.

We need to think and problem solve MORE like a coder. This means looking at issues and solutions with a data-driven/ data-led viewpoint using a systematic programming approach to solving problems. Adding this to our problem-solving toolbelt allows us to help design and create technology solutions to mitigate risks better and create more effective programs. Challenge process or control you see and ask; can this be digitized? If so, then can it be automated? If yes, then can we apply A.I. to this to make it better?

It still amazes me that up to half of an MLROs job today still involves routine and tedious manual tasks, which is a waste of time and energy for such a vital resource. We need to do LESS of the mundane manual tasks and find ways to digitize then automate them. The goal is to ultimately do only the highest value-adding manual tasks, mainly in critical thinking and complex problem-solving."

JOHN FOGARTY: "The first is that adaptability is critical. At CBA, we like to use the phrase 'manage the risk' instead of 'administer the risk.' Too often, we fall into habits of blindly following a process for the sake of completing the process (ticking the box) when we need to effectively manage the risk in front of us by managing it to the best outcome. This is what I mean by being adaptable. Generally, in my career, I have always said common sense will get you far, and applying it to most situations we face with a curious mindset will get you to the right answer.

Secondly, I would suggest understanding, at least at a basic level, coding or programming. My current Chief Risk Officer purchased all his staff 'Python for Dummies,' and I have to say it was fascinating and educational at the same time. In a world dominated by data and technology, it is extremely useful for our roles today and the future."

SCOTT BURTON: "Ongoing learning and understanding future trends is critical. With COVID-19, this will become even more relevant as technology adoption will undoubtedly accelerate. Learning and development can be completed in a number of ways, by online reading, industry seminars (online with COVID-19), networking by speaking to industry peers and generally being inquisitive and asking questions."

MARTIN JAMES WALLIS: "I think remaining curious. Understanding why something is being carried out the way it is can be a powerful enabler alongside the ability to challenge. In FinTech, the pace of development can be very fast, and if you are not interested in what is going on, it can very quickly pass you by. There are courses that can provide foundational knowledge, such as Elements of AI from the University of Helsinki, a great intro to AI course that is free. These intro courses will help take in where these technologies fit in the big picture; they may also provide you a pathway to further develop your learning and shift your current opinion. Another aspect with any new process or tech, whether building or implementing, is to make sure that you measure and test the outcomes before rolling out any new initiatives. The technologies are meant to speed up processes and help decisions, so speaking with the engineers and developers, making sure they understand why they are building or training them also plays an integral part. By combining these elements, you can hopefully sidestep some of the teething issues you may get with the adoption of something new."

PATRICIA SULLIVAN: "Make a serious study of how new payment methods, including Virtual Asset Service Providers, operate. The payments space is changing rapidly, and coming up to speed on these new players will enable you to understand better how/if ML or AI could be deployed to manage risk."

NICK TURNER: "I say let the machines take the tedious and boring work. I want the interesting stuff. Making judgments, communicating with other humans, persuading, and connecting are things computers cannot do. I think A.I. will give us more information we can use to enjoy our work."

DEBORAH YOUNG: "Firstly, this must be led from the top with a commitment to systemic stability and the consumer.

A well-informed Board and executive is a must, as well as the people who can impact widespread change. The decision to equip line managers with the right RegTech tools to manage the risks must be made to use A.I., machine learning, NLP, or blockchain.

There must be a deep understanding of the risks and complete alignment on these as an organization.

An organization must consider this alignment, including other areas of the organization that are important to the onboarding of new technologies such as I.T. security, Procurement, Innovation, Compliance, Risk, Strategy, and Legal.

Importance of your local RegTech Association and the role of regulators

They should consider organizations like The RegTech Association or other regional RegTech bodies as a primary port of call to unpack the opportunities. Associations – most often non-profit and non-aligned, will represent many firms that can be searched via online directories, risk-focused showcase programs, education initiatives, and conferences. Be engaged with your local regulators and attend their various forums to be informed on their commitment to and their expectations of your RegTech program."

JESSICA HODSON: "I think the easiest answer to this is curiosity. This will be, and is, a continuously growing and evolving space. The experts from last year, aren't always the experts this year so make sure you ask questions.

Make sure to be reflective and challenge yourself and your thinking questions such as "is this important technology, or are we using it to be more "tech".

Aside from this, buddy up with those IT nerds in your firm, or in your network. There is a real need for them and they will be the ones to drive and innovate change. This is going to be a very important market in the coming years."

MARTA LIA REQUEIJO:

Manage the expectations of relevant stakeholders

- It is as important to speak about the capabilities of these technologies as it is to speak about their limitations. Technology is not the silver bullet that will sort out all gaps and issues; technology is just a tool within a set of systems and controls, which, when combined, will enable us to achieve our aims.

Understand the technology

- Preventing and detecting financial crime with these technologies requires a new skill set that some financial crime compliance areas may not have at the moment: maintaining oversight of the models, correcting biases, and reviewing outcomes to understand if models are well-calibrated. To successfully deploy these technologies, it is critical to have the right people involved as early as possible and to limit the reliance on vendors/consultants - never retaining the knowledge within the organization.

Question 8: "If financial crime fighters want to stay relevant in this coming age of AI and machine learning technologies, what do you think are the most important steps for them to take?"

Understand the role that data quality and data governance play

- Data is fundamental. Multiple data sources across the business feed financial crime systems. Firms may not fully understand which data is being fed into their solutions or how the (lack of) quality of data impacts how the technology performs.

Align with the firm's strategy

- Ask yourself: do the technology solutions meet business needs today, and will they adapt to meet the firm's future business needs?

JOHN CUSACK: "Apart from making sure you vote for taxation of machines to create a level playing field for humans, from who they learn and may replace, you better be at least one step ahead.

Machine learning allows predictability and consistency, which are important elements we try to generate across large financial Crime programs, where human performance is very variable and may be unpredictable.

Most of the proof of concepts I have seen, though, are focussed mainly on large scale activities that have grown to levels that are unsustainable (and fall into the category of work where less should be done or it should really be automated) and so will affect this work more than most. That's no consolation to those employed in these tasks today, of course.

Suppose you look at today's automobile industry versus the one of yesteryear where humans manned the assembly line, which has been replaced with skilled humans interacting with programmed machines, managed by humans designed, tested, and marketed by humans. That this hasn't happened yet tells more about the inability to set up financial crime programs and maintain them to strict requirements such that processes can operate over time consistently. With laws, regulations, assurance, auditors, regulators, monitors all having a view on what's expected, it's no surprise fighting financial crime needs flexible humans to navigate the complexity and inconsistencies rife in the system."

STEVENSON MUNRO: "Despite all the discussion around A.I. and advances in technology, it amazes me that the way we combat financial crimes relies on technology that's basically 40 years old. Consider sanctions compliance: it's built around screening data sets against lists. The limitations of watchlist screening are well-known and long debated. Still, the solutions have been focused on advances in reducing false alerts, fuzzy logic, consistency and reliability in the watchlists, and efficiency in the process of screening. There's not been work to consider how A.I. and advances in technology might transform the fundamentals of how we detect and prevent sanctioned parties from accessing economic resources and financial services.

KYC is another example where the progress in identification and verification have focused on efficiencies and consistency in the process, but the fundamentals of knowing a client and what that means haven't advanced.

To stay relevant and effective in detecting and preventing financial crime to address the advances in technology and typologies, we need to recognize no one segment can transform on its own, and we will have to think beyond the existing methods."

ROD FRANCIS: "Education is the key. At least a basic understanding of Robot Process Automation (and its application) is critical. Effective application of Machine Learning (ML) is becoming more prevalent. We are still to see the real application of Artificial Intelligence (AI) that replicates human thinking in risk decisioning.

Do not forget that you must understand your traditional technology as it relates to your existing program. Do you understand how your client risk scoring model works? Do you really understand which TM scenarios you are running and why and how your initial/optimized thresholds have been set? Do you know your screening technology?

It's easy to focus on the new buzz words – AI/ML. Understand how your current technology works!

Being tech-savvy is now a critical component to being a Compliance professional."

JASON HOLT: "Personally, I made a conscious decision to join a firm that has AI and machine learning at the heart of its business.

I had concluded that this was the best way for me to learn more about how these critical technologies worked in practice and where they could realistically be used today.

I don't think this approach would be necessary for everyone. There are many ways to become more familiar with these technologies, including

Question 8: "If financial crime fighters want to stay relevant in this coming age of AI and machine learning technologies, what do you think are the most important steps for them to take?"

through reading online articles, academic courses, and speaking to vendors. But you can also learn by doing, AI technology is freely available now on the internet, and there is nothing to prevent you from trying it out learning along the way (but I would suggest not in your work environment, though, at least until you have mastered it).

It is relevant here to note that while many firms talk about AI and claim to use it, studies have shown many do not; in fact, a study carried out by a London based Venture Capital Firm (MMC) in 2019 reported that 40 percent of European startups, that were classified as AI companies didn't actually use artificial intelligence in a way that was "material" to their businesses."

ANTHONY NAPPI: "Embrace technology; if the organization does not have the skills internally bring the appropriate talent in.

The bad guys are certainly investing in how to circumvent and get around the existing controls – it is important to use these new technologies to find the non-obvious correlations, bad actors, gaps in the controls, etc. the volume of transactions and regulatory requirements continues to grow, new mediums of exchange are being added – such as cryptocurrencies – these technologies are required to be able to stay ahead as manual processes are expensive, are not as effective and prone to error and manipulation."

DR. WILLIAM SCOTT GROB: "The internet started in 1983, and since then, it has been transforming human behavior. At that time, most companies and individuals conducted transactions person-to-person via delivery mail and cash. For far too long, the financial sector procrastinated on advancing the payment and core banking system built in the 1970s and 80s.

Artificial intelligence (AI) may have the same impact. Within the decade, we will find a new kind of technology-assisted way of living and working.

Marco Iansati and Karim Lakhani write that the economy will be naturally reconfigured as companies and their products move to digital. In their book, "Competing in the Age of AI," Iansati and Lakhani articulate that the digital operating model will transform the way we interact.

We can already see the signs of the forthcoming transformation with driverless cars and Amazon's Alexa. Imagine a world where AI helps us with every aspect of our lives. Digital banks are on the rise.

Financial services are ripe for this type of change.

The new technology will change how we interact with one another and how we do business. It will create a unique ecosystem. As a result, the compliance function will need to change too.

Financial crime fighters must take the following steps to stay relevant in this coming age of AI and machine learning:

- Understand the trajectory of these technologies on your work
- Be open to change
- Embrace continual learning and take courses on artificial intelligence, machine learning, and data analytics
- Develop investigative skills
- Find projects that will use these new skills and demonstrate proficiency.

We need to build a new type of investigator.

The evolution of investigative tools will extend into AML analytics and detection models, which will drive new insights into criminal behavior. Anti-financial crime technologists will deploy data mining techniques on big data to find hidden relationships within customer behaviors and suspicious activity.

Subsequently, it would help if you prepared for the change that will inevitably change payments systems, exchange methods, and information flow. Start with small steps. Pick up a book or watch a video. Understand the concepts, the terminology, and the tools.

The role of anti-financial crime professionals must adapt to the new landscape. We need more individuals who are versed in data mining, analytics, and programming. Our industry will pivot to the technology-savvy data analysts."

PAUL (PADDY) O'HARA: "Embrace it, learn everything you can about it; join a crypto-asset company, join a VB, put your hand up for any roles that cover these types of technology."

WILL BROWN: "In order to stay relevant financial crime fighters will need to invest in their own personal and career development. It will be critically important that they take a proactive approach to learning to ensure they're ahead of developments in the space. This may be in the form of external learning courses, continuing professional development, join-

Question 8: "If financial crime fighters want to stay relevant in this coming age of AI and machine learning technologies, what do you think are the most important steps for them to take?"

ing professional membership associations, and also seeking active mentorship. Engaging with thought leaders and engaging with their content such as posts, podcasts and conversations are invaluable.

Understanding which firms are engaging in more cutting-edge technological implementation will allow individuals to target more forward-thinking FCC functions for their own career development. If you don't actively work in the AML/FCC Technology space or wider Transaction Monitoring areas, it may be harder to get direct exposure to more innovative technologies. However, where you can make a difference is by consciously deciding to work for companies that are strategically advancing the FCC technological agenda.

We're typically seeing the Fintech arena taking advantage of new technology within Compliance as they don't have the legacy systems that often encumbers larger financial institutions with the attendant cost and complications of implementing or upgrading brand new systems. Because they have also been able to scale up new financial crime compliance functions from scratch, they've been able to take advantage of new systems and efficiencies that have been developed over the last 5 to 10 years."

JAIKUMAR (JAI) RAMASWAMY: "While much attention tends to be focused on the way that AI and machine learning can be used to improve the detection and prevention of financial crimes, this is only one aspect of technology that will impact financial crimes compliance. Over the past decade, we have seen software eat the world. More and more of our lives are impacted by algorithms — whether it is the products that we buy on Amazon, the movies we watch on Netflix, the news we read on Facebook, and the web pages we find on Google.

The information revolution has been slower to impact financial services, partially due to the conservative nature of banking and the regulatory moat which banking enjoys. Nevertheless, the digital revolution is increasingly making inroads into the provision of financial services, whether through credit scoring models, cybersecurity and fraud detection using AI, or the convergence of information and settlement enabled by distributed ledgers and blockchain technology. Criminals are increasingly adept at exploiting these new technologies to support illicit financial activity, and financial crime fighters will need to learn about the profound ways that these technologies are disrupting the delivery of financial services and creating new criminal typologies."

MEL GEORGIE B. RACELA: "With slight modification to my ECC strategy, I think financial crime fighters should do 'ECI,' namely:

Educate. The rapid evolution of technology has resulted in the increasing complexity of financial transactions and the modus operandi employed by criminal actors. Hence, AML/CTF professionals must keep abreast of technological developments and understand business models of emerging technology-driven sectors, such as electronic money issuers and VASPs. Criminals have also attempted to use virtual assets to obfuscate fund flows. This makes it essential to scrutinize FATF's introduction of the Travel Rule on Virtual Assets. With the help of regulatory technology solutions, FIUs, such as the AMLC, can gain more visibility on transacting parties in the virtual asset space. So, education does not cover only awareness of technological developments but also understanding the modus operandi and regulatory advancements.

Collaborate. Crime fighters need to recognize their limitations and, by doing so, realize the need for partnership. The criminals that we are fighting have vast resources, and it is only through collaboration, joint effort, and technology- and information-sharing, can we effectively counter them.

Invest. In general, technology, especially AI, plays the role of facilitator more than disruptor of AML/CTF processes. Various types of technology have resulted in more timely and accurate due diligence and transaction-monitoring processes. They have given rise to more fact-driven and adaptable models to predict suspicious behavior. Successful solutions in the regulatory technology space primarily leverage on process automation, machine-learning, and data analytics to deliver more timely, accurate, and intelligent customer and transaction insights. Regulatory technology solutions are wide-ranging, affecting the end-to-end AML/CTF process—from enhancing identity verification and the overall due diligence process during customer on-boarding to applying behavioral analytics in transaction-monitoring, to automating regulatory reporting, and to finally digitizing recordkeeping."

GUILLERMO HORTA: "Every financial crime fighter should get involved in the AI discussion now. We need to learn about how the data available in the world might help us to predict and identify suspicious patterns, rather than looking at statistical numbered based rules where an individual could ultimately behave consistently wrong without being detected."

Question 8: "If financial crime fighters want to stay relevant in this coming age of AI and machine learning technologies, what do you think are the most important steps for them to take?"

ABTAR RANDHAWA: "I am a keen follower of how A.I. is evolving and especially threat modeling tools that pick up key social media tags and threads to enable and intelligently assists analytics to quickly weave through the data outliers to pick up actual threats be it to individuals, corporate products susceptible to fraud or even the rigging the results of electoral votes."

CARLOS GARCIA PAVIA: "Three words: "Never stop learning." I should perhaps apologize to those who may have expected a very elaborated and specific response, but it is simple, staying relevant requires continuously enhancing our skill set. Never fall to the point of being in a comfort zone for an extended period. The moment your daily job becomes a repetitive routine, chances are that it may be automated, and you may find yourself without a job soon after.

Keep developing not only your technical abilities and know-how, but most importantly, pay attention to further developing your soft skills. Technology and knowledge are increasing at an amazingly rapid speed; none of us will be able to catch up with it. Hence, it is only natural for those of us who have been around for a long time to move on and enable the new generations to do what they do best, use technology and knowledge to their advantage and the advantage of our organizations.

Over time, our roles must transition from "dragging the pencil" to "ideating the transformation." This requires a commitment to developing our soft skills to be able to set a clear vision and strategic objectives for our organizations. We must clearly understand the businesses that we support and have clarity of their strategic goals for our vision to be well-aligned with that of our stakeholders.

On the other hand, we must stay well connected with Academic organizations and industry networks to have a perpetual talent pool from which we can draw the resources we need to execute our strategies. A word of caution here, the most brilliant resources may not always be the best resources to execute our strategies. It may sound contradictory but let me explain. The most brilliant resources may be very attracted to use the most sophisticated and cutting-edge tools and techniques to develop overly complex solutions; they may not be as interested or even disappointed if they are asked to use more mundane kinds of tools and techniques. Perhaps a resource that is not so brilliantly gifted will be a better fit to develop something exceptionally good with the tools that are available. Such a person may also be a better bet for long-term talent retention.

Our organizations must also be ready to provide opportunities for career development if we do not want to become just a training ground. Let me explain. I have seen organizations spending a good deal of time training and preparing FCC and FCR professionals, only to lost them to competitors who will reap the fruits of the training that these resources have received.

There may be many reasons for this to happen, but sadly, the most common are compensation and bad management. I trust that on the first one most of our companies do a good job to compensate employees, but people are often moved in exchange for a few more dollars. However, when it comes to bad management, none of our organizations should be willing to lose valuable talent due to bad managers.

All our organizations must keep a clear focus on driving proper behaviors through the execution of our duties. Managers should be well-prepared to nurture their employees to succeed and flourish in the organization. We should be role models not only for our teams but across teams. For us to stay relevant, it is essential to be able to lead highly effective and motivated teams fully engaged not only in the day-to-day business as usual but invested in the strategies that will propel our organizations in the future."

Question 8: "If financial crime fighters want to stay relevant in this coming age of AI and machine learning technologies, what do you think are the most important steps for them to take?"

How can you apply these lessons and insights to your career or life today?

_____

_____

_____

_____

_____

_____

_____

_____

_____

_____

_____

_____

_____

Knowing what you now know, what are some mistakes you've made that you want other financial crime fighters to learn from or avoid?

QUESTION 9

TADEO (JUN) CLARAVALL: "Whenever I make a mistake, huge ones especially, I try not to engage in self-flagellation and instead look to learn a lesson and maybe even gain some wisdom from my mistake. I've made so many mistakes in my career, which could probably fill all the pages of this book. For the sake of brevity, I'll give 3. Not necessarily my top 3, just the three that come to mind right as I write this.

First, waiting too long to seek help.

Like most people, I always wanted to show the world that I am capable and self-reliant. When faced with problems, my old programming was to do whatever I can to fix them before seeking help. Now I realize how foolish that approach is. Sure, if the problem fits neatly within my sphere of expertise and I have the time, and it is my job to fix it, then I should do it. But what tended to happen in the past is that any problem brought to my attention, I would attempt to fix regardless of whether I am capable, have the time, or whether it is my job. I can now see not just how unproductive that was for me, how potentially destructive that was to my team, and how arrogant that must have appeared to others despite my best intentions at being helpful.

Now my strategy is first and always WHO, not HOW. Before starting to solve any problem, I ask who can help? Who has been through this before? Who has the expertise, the time, and the responsibility to help me with this problem? The only problem or task that I do nowadays are those that fall within my sphere of 'genius', which is certainly not big but is the area that I can be most effective at and enjoy doing simultaneously.

Second, my tendency to overthink things.

In my younger years, I would get myself tied in knots, ruminating about a problem. 'Researching' until I'm satisfied I know enough about the issue before taking action or making decisions. There is a place for this decision-making approach. For serious life or death matters, or if there could be significant consequences (e.g. jail time, significant fines, or reputational hit for my company), or if a decision is of the irreversible kind, then yes, follow this approach. However, over 95% of the challenges I faced didn't fall under this category: the result, unnecessary angst, stress, and delays in taking action.

Over time, I've gotten better at this. This decision-making lesson from American statesman, retired general, and former secretary of state Colin Powell helped me significantly; he called it his 40-70 rule. His rule states that "you need between 40 and 70 percent of the total information to make a decision. With less than 40 percent, you will likely make a poor choice, and with more than 70 percent, you will end up taking too long, and the decision will be made for you! The point is that all leaders should aspire to make more correct decisions than incorrect ones. But they cannot be so fearful of making mistakes that they make no decisions at all. There has to be a balance between perfection and speed. The truth is that you will never have all the information you need to make a perfect decision."

Third, putting my career ahead of my health and wellbeing.

This is hard to admit because it took three potentially dangerous health scares to make me realize my fault.

I consider myself a reasonably ambitious professional. I've always had high hopes and dreams concerning my career. I believe it's essential to have ambition. But if you couple this ambition with a punishing work schedule that included consistent late nights and working on weekends and doing this for over two decades took a toll on my health. Add to this my tendency to try and tackle problems by myself (mistake #1) and overthinking (mistake #2) led to three bad health events that physically, mentally, and emotionally beat me down to the point that I was out of commission for 2 to 3 weeks at a time and on one occasion had to stay in the hospital.

Nothing, I repeat, NOTHING should come ahead of taking care of your health and wellbeing. Certainly not work, and dare I say, not even relationships. Here's why. If you don't have your health, you're not only going to be useless at work; you could potentially be making significant mistakes in your decision-making. If you don't have your health, you're not going to be a helpful or loving husband, wife, partner, parent, friend, or colleague. You'll be irritable and no fun to be around.

Here's my advice which I've learned the hard way. Rest before you get tired. Take scheduled time off. Get sufficient sleep. Eat right. Exercise and move! There is so much good advice, strategies, and tactics on getting and maintaining good health out there. Pick one and do it!

One final word on self-care. A favorite author of mine, the late great Jim Rohn, once said, "Please take care of you for me, and I'll take care of me for you." Self-care is not selfish. On the contrary, it may be one of the most generous things you can do for yourself and others."

JOHN FOGARTY: "Being dogmatic is never helpful in the long run. Always listen to other opinions even if you have a strong view on a subject. It is better to hold your view lightly and be open to change than to hold it tightly and be ignorant and closed to other perspectives."

JOHN CUSACK: "Four things:

1) Taking a risk-based approach to compliance is only possible where the law allows a risk-based approach to compliance, and it's usually interpreted with the benefit of hindsight against your interpretation even if honestly and reasonably determined. So, document your rationale and tell everyone that's what you are doing, including the regulators.

2) Tax Evasion is a serious crime. Not as serious as drug trafficking or organized crime, but it's still a crime.

3) When you are in a senior position, don't wait too long to make the decisions you know you have to make. You may not be there as long as you think, and the opportunity may pass.

4) If you are successful, you will be around for a long time. So, make friends and keep in contact, not only when they can help you.

MARTIN JAMES WALLIS: "Don't assume and ask questions. It can be hard to demonstrate a lack of knowledge or understanding on your part, but ask when you don't know something, whether that is one of your colleagues, managers, someone within your peer network. We all start from a different point and learn in different ways, so use the available resources. You can also pay that back as you become more experienced."

STEVENSON MUNRO: "There is a lot of "group-think" in our profession. The careers focused on combatting financial crimes attract individuals with similar motivation and training. When I think about the mistakes I most regret, I can identify decisions or actions that could have

Question 9: "Knowing what you now know, what are some mistakes you've made that you want other financial crime fighters to learn from or avoid?"

123

gone differently and might have changed the outcome if I'd sought or actively engaged or didn't dismiss a challenging perspective. It's very easy to validate your own priorities and solutions – I've found that it's likely that your sounding board on any particular problem will reflect your own thinking. While that might be comforting and help propel actions, we miss things, and we limit our ability to transform.

The response to group-think might seem obvious, but, at least for me, it's not easy. I have to deliberately and consciously recognize when I'm frustrated or annoyed or bristling at a decision, an approach, a problem, a comment, or a question; and then, instead of reacting (often to explain why I disagree), to pause myself and force myself to ask a question to understand what someone else is seeing and thinking through. This takes time that we seldom feel like we have, sometimes a lot of time.

I also think it's important to regularly look around your team and your go-to colleagues to check that you've sought out and built teams and relationships with individuals who have different backgrounds and experiences and perspectives – and not just to a "devil's advocate," but to embed diversity and ingrain inclusion."

MEL GEORGIE B. RACELA: "This is not so much a personal mistake but a collective lapse from which the Philippines and, perhaps, other countries have learned lessons from. It is a lesson not to leave any stone unturned. In 2016, the casino sector was not subject to AML/CTF framework, and so the Bangladesh Bank cyber-heist happened.

As with any large case, said unfortunate incident had significant effects on the country's legal and regulatory framework as additional measures to strengthen the AML/CTF regime in the Philippines were taken. More important, the better takeaway is that all financial institutions are constantly under attack by hackers, so it is crucial to prioritize cybersecurity."

PATRICIA SULLIVAN: "Two things I would highlight. First, while it is a cliché, I believe you will excel if you love what you are doing. I love the fighting financial crime arena and spend my 'free' time in this space. FCC may not be for you, and that's OK and an opportunity to find your true passion. Second, if you find yourself in a situation where your manager doesn't support you, and you know/feel /smell it when you're in it, then don't waste precious months or years in that situation. Make every effort to find a new opportunity. There have been points in my career where I didn't heed the above advice, and I can't get that time back."

ROD FRANCIS: "I learned reasonably early on in my career that you need to create an organization and surround yourself with people that are better than you and then provide them with the environment, support and leadership to realize their full potential and achieve the goals of the organization."

JESSICA HODSON: "Somewhat controversially I think becoming a specialist can sometimes close of avenues, rather than open them.

If you're really passionate about sanctions for example, do that and certainly specialise but try not to do so at a detriment to your more holistic financial crime knowledge.

Spend time working with your AML teams, or wider business to understand how sanctions is a cog in a wider financial crime risk assessment. People who can view a financial crime task with a wider lens, usually get the better result."

GUILLERMO HORTA: "Getting more involved with lawmakers and legislators during the issuance of reviewed AML or Financial Crime rules. It is imperative to make sure that lawmakers understand how a Bank works and how the products of a Bank can be used to disguise illicit proceeds. Such knowledge should be based on thorough analysis, not on one tale or experience from a law enforcement agent who testified a single case with a defined pattern. I agreed that criminals might follow the easiest ways but thinking that criminals typically use only cash or having the mentality that criminals only disguise themselves behind a casino or an MSB is obsolete. Organized crime members are much better than that."

ABTAR RANDHAWA: "Many mistakes but the one mistake that I would avoid would be not focusing attention on the "big ticket" items and challenging the status quo until the right outcome is achieved. Complexities exist in performing our roles, and the challenges of 'doing the right thing' with the desired outcome can on occasion be lost in the myriad of organizations and the views and opinions of many experts. Having a clear sense of purpose and conviction in your own thoughts and your very own success measures will help provide the focus required to navigate issues and make them stick within organizations. The amount of time, effort, and intelligent thought performed to analyze data, processes, procedures, and policies is a unique skill and, therefore, should never be underplayed. Keeping that in mind and being able to explain and rationalize your ap-

Question 9: "Knowing what you now know, what are some mistakes you've made that you want other financial crime fighters to learn from or avoid?"

125

proach will, in most occasions, alleviate any concerns stakeholder may have in your approach of arriving at your conclusions."

PAUL (PADDY) O'HARA: "Work in a company where your values are aligned. If you wake up in the morning and don't want to go to work, it's time to find something else."

CARLOS GARCIA PAVIA: "In my younger years, I used to think that if I was particularly good at doing something, I should make sure to keep doing it rather than teaching others how to do it. After all, having unique knowledge goes hand to hand with job security, isn't it? If you are nodding in agreement with me, I must tell you that you are as wrong as I was.

Keeping knowledge to yourself may not only give you a false sense of job security, but it will also serve as a very heavyweight that will drag you away from progressing your career. If there is no one ready in your team to take over for you with minimum disruption, then you are basically condemned to keep doing your function for years to come. No promotion, no significant pay increase, nothing new to do on the horizon. Others, probably less qualified, may be able to progress their careers more rapidly because the organization can afford to move them onto different roles without causing disruption.

Being the only one able to do something in your team creates a great burden for you and your family. Not only your workload may become overwhelming to the point of going on sleepless nights and restless weekends, but you will end up completely burned out very quickly. It is an unsustainable burden for you and for your organization. Have you heard about the "key person risk"? That is right, it exists, and when it comes to regulatory functions such as in FCC or FCR, it must be mitigated at the earliest.

The moral of the story is to always have a good managerial succession plan in place, not only for you but for the staff reporting to you. You never know when the next good opportunity will come across, so you need to always be ready to jump into a new role at any given time. Sometimes you will be asked to double or triple hat or to act as an interim replacement for someone. At that point, you should be able to have someone in your team ready to help you fill-up the gaps or to replace you completely in your core function. There is nothing wrong with this; you will not lose your job if someone else can do it. If you remain relevant and able to deliver not only on what you are paid for but beyond that, you will be ok.

Your goal should be to consistently exceed the expectations of your function, to become a top performer and a role model for your organization. Be the first person that comes to mind for your boss and your boss's boss when they need someone to help resolve higher complexity problems or to effectively drive strategic initiatives. Be part of the elite group of resources that are known by their capacity to adapt and to execute flawlessly under highly dynamic conditions. Recognize and shout the achievements of your team, praise the extraordinary talents that everyone brings to the table. Share the success and take accountability for the mistakes. Yes, we all make mistakes at some point, and we should learn from them. Mistakes are part of being human, never let the fear of making a mistake stop you from making decisions. Carefully consider all variables and the consequences before deciding, but never be frozen in fear. Most of all, if someone in your team makes a mistake, please avoid finger-pointing, avoid hunting for culprits. Instead, make a collective and conscious analysis of what went wrong, identify how the problem may have been prevented, and include the lessons learned as part of your playbook."

JAIKUMAR (JAI) RAMASWAMY: "Clear communication is one of the most important skills of financial crime professionals. My biggest mistakes have typically involved not communicating clearly the reasons for making a particular recommendation, whether about a client relationship or developing a product or service. I have found that I have the least influence when resorting to expertise and authority and, conversely, more when clearly explaining the risks of taking a particular course of action. Additionally, I have typically found that one of the most effective ways of convincing stakeholders is to provide an alternative course of action — a "no" is less effective than a "no, but..."

In general, I have found that most stakeholders I have dealt with do not want to do the wrong thing but need to know the risks of what they would like to do and available alternatives before they make a decision. Another related mistake involves lacking humility — you should always be open to being wrong. There have been many times in my career where I have gone into a meeting planning to recommend one course of action, and have been surprised to learn new facts that led me to change my thinking. In short, at its best, financial crime fight requires making sure that you understand all the facts, clearly explaining the risks involved and providing solution-oriented options."

How can you apply these lessons and insights to your career or life today?

_____

_____

_____

_____

_____

_____

_____

_____

_____

_____

_____

_____

_____

Is there any one mistake you find financial crime fighters making over and over in their careers?

QUESTION 10

TADEO (JUN) CLARAVALL: "From the perspective of a financial crime practitioner working in the private sector and the second line of defense, the one mistake I see us making over and over is our lack of proper understanding of the businesses, products, and services that our company offers. This creates two key challenges.

First, most of us understand financial crime risks and the financial crime laws, rules, and regulations that apply to our companies. Still, our lack of proper understanding of the business, products, and services results in a tendency to become overly conservative in our assessment of risk, and this reflects in the unduly restrictive advice we provide to the business or, worse, an incomplete or incorrect evaluation of risk resulting in poor advice that can lead to disastrous outcomes.

Second, not fully understanding businesses, products, and services results in delays when assessing risk and issuing our advice. To do our jobs correctly, we need to gather product information and discuss process flows and models with the business before giving advice. Having a solid business, product, and service knowledge beforehand means that only discussions around deviations or modifications to our understanding of the business are needed before giving advice.

Taking steps to get better at understanding businesses, products and services will not only make us more effective and efficient at our work, but it might also help enhance our relationship with the business people as it affords us and the opportunity to meet and converse at regular intervals and not only need to meet at times when there's a financial crimes issue or when product/ deal approvals are required."

PATRICIA SULLIVAN: "Not having an opinion and not knowing where their lines are. It is tough to assess each client, deal, or transaction and not operate within a defined risk appetite that you are very clear about in isolation. When the tough business call comes on a late Friday afternoon when you are trying to get out of the office or on the eve of the holiday, your likelihood of making the right call with the right mitigants increases if you know where your lines are."

WILL BROWN: "One consistent mistake I see from a recruitment perspective is in the choices that candidates make when they move roles and the thought process which drives these.

In 2013/2014, we saw a massive increase in the overall global size of FCC functions in many of the global banks. This suddenly gave a lot of FCC professionals the opportunity to get title promotions and large salary increases on an annual basis for the first time and on a grand scale. This was particularly evident in geographic locations that had small populations of FCC individuals coupled with increasing regulatory pressure (Hong Kong would be one example). This meant that candidates were being promoted more quickly, often with only a years' worth of experience which is generally insufficient to fully embed yourself in an organization and successfully complete or build a complex project.

As a result, the candidate pool became bloated from a title and salary perspective but did not reflect the requisite skillsets to justify these costs.

Obviously, every individual has the right (and should push) to be fairly compensated for the work that they do. That should, however, be commensurate to their experience and impact in the business.

As FCC teams in key city locations such as NYC and London have shrunk from 2017 onwards in the larger global banks, what we now see is that there is a large over-compensated candidate pool who have been forced, through various offshoring/nearshoring and attrition-based strategies, to make moves that they wouldn't necessarily have wanted to make. These would either be to institutions without the right platform or culture to make them successful or simply a role in an area they didn't want to pursue.

I believe the key factor that should be taken into consideration when making a move is whether the institution where you're going to work will give you the best platform to succeed. This will be dictated by their internal culture's attitude towards Financial Crime Compliance, whether they have the budget to hire the best teams and whether you have a manager who will give you the right direction to succeed. With these factors changing every 2/3 years or so as programs are built out before becoming more "BAU," candidates should focus on how this 2/3-year career move will best set you up to achieve your next goal beyond it.

Question 10: "Is there any one mistake you find financial crime fighters making over and over in their careers?"

131

Job moves should align with what you want to achieve from a medium and long-term viewpoint allowing you to build up a story of success which is crucial in managing your own career."

NICK TURNER: "Don't get stuck in a compliance silo. The most valuable information I've gained in my career has come from pestering colleagues in operations and I.T. to teach me how things work.

It's one thing to know a regulation or a rule. It's another to be able to give some detail about how it applies in practice."

JOHN CUSACK: "Not especially. I have found them more dedicated than lawyers and compliance officers and driven by a personal mission, which is a positive. Some are too driven by titles and compensation, move around too much, and can't settle, worry me most. Gathering first-class experiences and working with high-quality people should be the focus. The titles and compensation will come then if you deserve it."

JASON HOLT: "Too often people focus purely on the laws and regulations without appropriate regard for or knowledge of the specific purpose they were created for.

Without an understanding of the risk they were designed to mitigate, it is extremely difficult to ensure they are interpreted and applied correctly, especially in the fintech environment. Moreover, this context or "the why", is precisely what business management are desperate to understand, so they can help ensure that the controls they have in their businesses are actually dealing with the real risk, rather than being the result of a policy designed for one business line being applied inappropriately to another.

As a fantastic manager of mine, I always remember financial crime compliance officers used to say – "The keepers of the why".

JEROME MICHAILIDIS: "At times, I think said fighters take too long to make a decision. It's important to collaborate and consider, but there are often times when decisions need to be made more quickly, based on the information available. One can amend the decision later, but it's hard to make up for time lost with no decision."

JOHN FOGARTY: "Yes, just following a process for the sake of process. You have to know why you do what you do! Understanding this will enable you to apply effective judgment and common sense to the risks you are managing – Adaptability!"

ABTAR RANDHAWA: "Listening is key. I am a firm believer in understanding the challenges and solutions being conveyed by respective experts and how each of these is enabling financial crime fighters to garner extensive and multiple sources of knowledge with the added advantage of being skilled and experienced enough to be able to join the dots.

Having the horizontal and lateral view of a process or a program of work coupled with an undiluted lens free from any prejudice or influence. This is the point when you can make a clear judgment call and see a process end to end with full knowledge of all component parts coupled with risk experience should enable the good auditor to conclude on whether the solution is fit for purpose. This, in my opinion, is the key to the role of a highly-skilled auditor and risk professional."

JESSICA HODSON: "Not the most common one, but certainly the one which I see having the most reactionary effect: conversations around pay rises, lateral moves, or progression. So many people know the work they do is important, so assume this will be rewarded, and if it's not, it leaves them feeling undervalued, and then they leave!

You need to talk about your career and development sometimes in a more direct way than you want to. Conversely, though, be very honest with how hard you work, and level-wise where you are – every person I talk to seems to think they are at the top level for their banding, remind yourself there are always growth areas.

You should have this career conversation before you want to leave, and don't always expect the answer you want. If the answer is no to pay rises, you can always ask, "what can I do between now and xx to help me get a raise."

GUILLERMO HORTA: "I think a common mistake is not having the right

people in the right roles. I have seen very senior roles in Financial Crime Fighting that are occupied by people that lack a true financial crime career experience. A restaurant manager might be great for a specific business, but that same manager might not necessarily be the best manager for a food chain. The same situation happens at Banks. We con-

Question 10: "Is there any one mistake you find financial crime fighters making over and over in their careers?"

133

stantly see someone with good business acumen and common sense, but no AML or true global or international experience occupying Global Financial Crime positions."

MEL GEORGIE B. RACELA: "The tendency to be complacent and be unresponsive to the times. Financial crime evolves because criminals continue to find ways to launder their proceeds. That is why we need to continuously educate, collaborate, and commit."

ARMINA ANTONIOU: "I think many of us have made the mistake of assuming that all of our colleagues understand what we do and why we do it. For this reason, change management, training, and communications with our colleagues, particularly frontline staff, is really important.

Any change to processes or systems that will affect front line staff or any staff outside of the risk & compliance teams needs to have the proper change management attention paid to it – whether this is in the form of specific training and education or communications tailored to each team or input into processes from frontline staff that takes into account operational difficulties or quirks of the particular environment. The messages about change need to be delivered practical and relevant to those impacted by Anti-Financial Crime processes, procedures, systems, or policies.

This is why we try to use real examples or stories to explain to others what we do and why we do it. I completely understand when business people are confronted with a new way of doing things or new restrictions on what they can do because of new regulatory feedback or updated AML/CFT regulations.

A common frustration among people who don't work in Risk or compliance is "We have never had to do that before" or "We have never had a problem with that before." It's true – not everyone has been in trouble with the regulators in relation to financial crime compliance, and not all corporates have ever been exposed to financial crimes.

I think of it as very similar to seat belt use and car crash prevention. It makes no sense to wait until you have been in a car crash to start using a seat belt, which can prevent or reduce injury in the unlikely event your car is in an accident. As a society, we have heeded medical and scientific advice, and largely all of us wear a seat belt when we get into a vehicle. In most countries, there is also legislation in place to make seat belt wearing mandatory. It is for this reason that it doesn't make sense to wait until you have, or your employer has been affected directly by financial crimes to take steps to prevent or detect such activity."

CARLOS GARCIA PAVIA: "Perhaps the most common mistake that financial crime fighters often make is to invest so much time, and effort in the detection and post-detection stages of our FCC/FCR processes to achieve efficiency gains, instead of pushing and influencing data remediation strategies that may help resolve much of the inefficiencies.

Yes, all our organizations have data quality issues, we all have data gaps, data is imperfect. It should not be an excuse not to do anything to remediate it. We all know that bad data drives bad processes and derives potentially bad outcomes. Some organizations may be very aware of their data blemishes but may decide not to invest in remediating them as there may not be a clear understanding of the return on investment that such remediation may bring.

Really? One must be blind not to appreciate that remediating data is not only important to run FCC/FCR processes that deliver a better outcome in the form of increased effectiveness and operational efficiency, but remediating data is also key to maximize our opportunities to automate the alert adjudication stage of these processes.

While these two benefits go directly to the bottom-line, remediating data may also provide a boost to revenue-generating initiatives if we consider that businesses will have access to better analytics to identify and promote more profitable products onto healthier and less risky customer segments to keep building long-lasting relationships with our customers.

I think it is also worth highlighting that many of our organizations may not yet be leveraging the highly valuable intelligence that our operations teams add to the alerts on adjudication. Teams that are used to add well-redacted notes to describe the rationale of their adjudication decisions are delivering essential information to boost automation of alert adjudication. There is a wealth of actionable intelligence that can be mined through today's technologies to learn, emulate and scale the actions from our operations analysts. This has to be properly governed and supervised, though, as analysts may make mistaken decisions from time to time, and we don't want our smart processes to learn and repeat those mistakes.

Unsupervised Artificial Intelligence and Machine Learning techniques may not be the right approach for processes related to FCC/FCR as organizations may lose the ability to clearly understand and explain the outcome of those processes. If left unsupervised, these techniques may jeopardize the integrity and effectiveness of our processes through making wrong decisions derived from flawed learnings. This may be especially dangerous when it comes to processes that require speed and accuracy, such as sanctions screening, even more important when it comes to transaction screening.

This is perhaps a good time to talk about the often disparity of focus, investment, and effort between the Transaction Monitoring and the Screening processes. Historically our organizations have spent much more time and money on our transaction monitoring programs than on our screening programs. Some organizations seem to be missing the point that the risk involved in making a mistaken decision in screening may have far more serious consequences than not raising a defensive SAR.

Failure to generate a sanctions-related alert in screening means that our organizations may be inadvertently processing transactions that should not have been executed or that we may have customers in our portfolios that we should not have. Some organizations have already seen and experience the consequences of such failures in the form of hefty penalties and, in the worst case, cease and desist orders imposed on their businesses. Given the very astringent sanctions regulations, sanctions screening is a high-risk sport; it requires speed and flawless accuracy, it requires perfection, it requires continuous innovation and continuous investment to keep it at the top of its game all the time.

Transaction monitoring, on the other hand, is rather a game of behavioral statistics. No, I am not diminishing its relevance or importance; it is absolutely a must-have. I may be oversimplifying it with the intention of putting it into perspective. In TM, the goal is to identify transactions that may be considered suspicious due to a variety of reasons (exceeded thresholds, unforeseen or unexpected behavior in our customer segmentation, etc.). All of which happens after transactions are executed, not before. There is nothing we can do or should do to stop or prevent those transactions. All we do is to report the suspicious transactions through SARs that go to federal regulators for analysis, and ultimately some of them will constitute cases ending up with federal law enforcement authorities for prosecution. The federal authorities make the ultimate call of what to prosecute and what not.

In contrast, in sanctions screening, our organizations must make the ultimate call to prevent the on-boarding of bad actors as customers or to exit those relationships if they are already in. Our organizations are expected to freeze assets or reject transactions in the event of a true match. Financial institutions are expected to prevent those transactions from being executed and to report the same to the corresponding federal authorities. It is a real-time game. Do you appreciate the difference now? My hope is that putting this into perspective, the FCC/FCR decision-makers across financial institutions are influenced to shift their focus and devote the funding and resources that are needed to keep screening permanently at the top of its game."

PAUL (PADDY) O'HARA: "Don't chase the money and flit from firm to firm. You won't have time to be really happy and do work that you're really proud of. If you work hard and put your hand up for everything, the reward will eventually come. But don't stay forever, either!!"

MAGGIE QIU: "One common mistake I saw is that financial crime fighters often walk the walk, but not talk the talk. I mean that they often are hardworking people but often not paying attention to the importance of communication. Whether it is to explain to regulators and auditors or educate and discuss with internal stakeholders, they are not always good at telling the stories and articulating the risks in a direct, in an easy-to-understand manner."

How can you apply these lessons and insights to your career or life today?

_____

_____

_____

_____

_____

_____

_____

_____

_____

_____

_____

_____

_____

_____

_____

What failures have you learned
from the most that have
contributed to your
career success?

QUESTION 11

TADEO (JUN) CLARAVALL: "A disastrous failure on my first attempt at public speaking.

In my first year working, I was given an opportunity to do some public speaking at a work event. I was excited and prepared well. But I crashed and burned. I memorized my lines, made no connection with the audience. I was boring. It was so bad that the next day I overheard a senior executive of the bank telling another colleague that I was probably the worst public speaker he'd ever seen. I was crushed.

I remember brooding over this failure for many weeks and embarrassed to show my face at the office. Ultimately, I got over it, and instead of swearing off public speaking forever, I decided to get good at it. I learned everything I needed to know about public speaking. I read books (there was no Youtube in 1994) and practiced harder, so the next time I'm given an opportunity, I will prove to myself and others that I am an excellent public speaker.

Throughout my 25-year career, I've since spoken several hundreds of times publicly to audiences of five to five hundred people from all over the world. Sure, I still had some bad experiences once or twice, but over 99% of the time, the talk, presentation, or training I conducted was effective, enjoyable, and well-received.

I believe that my ability to speak on my feet, to move and inspire audiences to take action, has done more to help my career progress than perhaps any other skill that I have developed.

Lesson: Early failures, if seen as a learning opportunity, can catapult you to levels of success in that very thing if you do not give up and instead use the failure event as motivation to act and improve."

MATT FRIEDMAN: "When I was 28 years old, I worked for an organization that evaluated US-funded international development health contractors around the world. While my job was to collect information for evaluation assignments, before long I was invited to participate in some of these events. I went from serving as a support person to being an active member of the evaluation team. I often entered a country, reviewed the operational plan, and made determinations about the impact of the work being done. Over a two-year period, I traveled to more than 20 countries.

The red carpet was rolled out for me, and I was often treated like a king. The thing is, when you evaluate a major development project, your decisions can determine the fate of a multi-million-dollar program. A company's future can sometimes hang in the balance. For this reason, those being evaluated went out of their way to please the evaluators. That was the way things were.

Being young and inexperienced, I allowed this fawning to go to my head. The more evaluations I carried out, the more full of myself I became. At the same time, I learned how to manage the system to easily get the assignments I wanted. My arrogance was off the chart. I believed myself to be a golden boy destined to climb to the top. There was no restraining my unbridled ambition. When I became a contender for a major promotion, I realized that I needed some long-term, in-country field experience to remain competitive. Accordingly, I took a 24-month fellowship in Nepal.

Within six months, I came to realize that despite what I had originally thought, I was a terrible evaluator. It wasn't that I didn't know how to collect the information, analyze it, and then write up an acceptable report. That part was easy. The problem was that, as an evaluator, I'd fly in and out of a country without spending enough time to understand the nuances and complexity of the process required to implement a project in a field setting. I had failed to comprehend the internal and external politics, the endless administrative delays, the interagency power struggles, the interference by government, and the logistical issues. It is impossible to understand the extent of these factors until you are faced with them in a real-life situation.

While I was supposed to be in Nepal for two years, I was so humbled by the experience that I stayed there for eight. During this time, I did all I could to gain a deeper understanding of the cross-cultural development setting.

I learned from my failure as an evaluator that it is important for young people to understand that we often leave university believing that we have all the answers. We sometimes view those who are senior to us as being slow and simple-minded. This comes from allowing logic and common

Question 11: "What failures have you learned from the most that have contributed to your career success?"

141

sense, instead of experience, to become our guide. In this case, the best thing that can happen is a situation where our arrogance and inexperience can be revealed. Understanding the importance of humility is one of the most valuable lessons any of us can learn. Fortunately, I learned this early in my career."

JEROME MICHAILIDIS: "In our field, one always has to have alternate solutions. Even if you are steadfast on backing 'choice A', you have to already consider choices B and C in case things don't work out."

MARTIN JAMES WALLIS: "That failure is an opportunity to learn. In the Instagram world of today, everyone and their lives are perfect, and that is not real, well not in my world. Not everything will work out, and being resilient enough to work through and understand why it didn't work means that the failure will hopefully not develop into a failing. I think this is something that the military has learned to do very well. There are many scenarios where things don't go right, but you must adapt to the situation to achieve your objectives. It is no different in the world of anti-financial crime and being open to different perspectives, different ways of working, and being challenged on your ideas and plans. This should mean that you have anticipated some of the problems before they occur and are mentally prepared to work around these to iterate, revise, or even start again to reach your goals."

MEL GEORGIE B. RACELA: "As mentioned, after the Bangladesh Bank cyber-heist in 2016, the AMLC took measures to strengthen the AML/CTF regime in the country. This includes, among other things, the following:

- Passage of RA 10927 or An Act Designating Casinos as Covered Persons under RA No. 9160, otherwise known as the Anti-Money Laundering Act of 2001, as amended;
- Issuance of the 2018 Implementing Rules and Regulations, Rules of Procedure in Administrative Cases, and other key regulations;
- AMLC Secretariat reorganization;
- Enhanced international cooperation with counterpart FIUs;
- Enhanced domestic cooperation and coordination with law enforcement agencies and other government agencies;
- Improved outreach to banks and money service businesses; and

- Conduct of AML/CTF trainings and accreditation of AML/CTF trainers to increase awareness among the covered persons of their obligations under the AMLA, as amended

In addition, the AMLC has led the conduct and implementation of the following:

- Second National Risk Assessment Report, which is a government-wide evaluation of the overall exposure of the country to money laundering and its related predicate offenses, terrorism, and terrorism financing; and
- National AML/CFT Strategy, which has been approved by the President through Executive Order No. 68 and which is a co-ordinated approach for the government and the private sector in combating money laundering and terrorism financing in the country.

Further, the AMLC has recently endeavored to bolster the country's legal and supervisory framework by persistently campaigning for the passage of:

- The Anti-Terrorism Act of 2020 (ATA), which includes criminal provisions for foreign terrorist fighters as well as a designation process pursuant to the requirements of United Nations Security Council Resolution No. 1373 and the FATF; and
- RA 11521, which amends the AMLA, includes offshore gaming operators, real estate developers, brokers as covered persons, and tax crimes as a predicate offense.

I consider these as several highlights of being the Secretariat's Executive Director."

GUILLERMO HORTA: "A Financial Crimefighter should have the passion to learn on a daily basis and the courage to challenge any position that can put a financial institution at risk. Being able to speak up and have the ability to communicate with impact are key elements for a successful career."

NICK TURNER: "I spent a lot of time in my early 20's trying to do jobs that other people found interesting, but that wasn't for me. Thankfully, I learned how to write well in my early career, and that has been my number one skill ever since."

Question 11: "What failures have you learned from the most that have contributed to your career success?"

143

ANTHONY NAPPI: "The biggest mistake I made early in my career was staying in a very similar job for far too long. I went from managing a North American operation to doing the same role effectively but only on a global basis.

While it improved my management and oversight skills, I would have been better served to do an entirely different role, so to have expanded my knowledge base.

As I was young in my career, I could have gone into another discipline such as credit risk or treasury which are skills that have universal applicability and would have made me a more well-rounded senior leader."

ABTAR RANDHAWA: "Many people are saying the same thing but use different terminology and levels of sophisticated language to express essentially the same idea or concept. Keeping things simple and explainable to the layman is a constant challenge. However, overcoming the challenges will hold everyone in good stead, especially when working on or leading transformational programs of work, such as remediation activities across multiple jurisdictions that are complex due to systems, processes, and controls."

JESSICA HODSON: "I think the biggest mistake I have made is underestimating the power of communication, and I am also seeing this internally within clients at the moment. Sometimes issues which start out small can quickly progress to larger problems – the mountain out of molehills!

With the new working from home allotments, I hear a lot about people grumbling around too much or not enough communication. Particularly when there is a change to policy or procedure.

I think we all know communication is important, but for me personally it was realising the impact internally of how much tone and delivery can impact the messages."

JOHN CUSACK: "It's likely you might be wrong, so the more smart, experienced people who feel free to disagree is the most important lesson. No matter what level you are at, there is always someone that can add something to your thinking and decision-making that will improve it. It is not always the hardest things that trip you up as these often go through more rigorous analysis and challenge but can be the things you can take for granted. You just don't see what your missing- other people will as they are looking at it in a way you will not appreciate unless you seek out their advice. Being wrong is not a sign of weakness. Being arrogant and pig-headed is."

CARLOS GARCIA PAVIA: "Undoubtedly, when I let go of doing all by myself to expedite deliverables, not only did I remove a very heavy-weight from my shoulders, but I started to prepare others to be equally capable to understand and resolve complex issues fast. This change gave me the scale to do more, to learn more, and to start doing more interesting, more intellectually rewarding tasks. I can say that I have learned much more in the past eight years than what I learned in over 20 years of my career before.

When I left Citi in 2013, my family, friends, and I considered it an extremely high-risk move. We all considered that most of my career was built on Citi-specific knowledge that may have been only valuable there. However, after joining LexisNexis Risk Solutions, I realized that the lessons I learned from my time at Citi were applicable across the financial services landscape in general.

This gave me the opportunity to learn about the use of big data to resolve FCC/FCR challenges. It gave me the opportunity to influence others through thought leadership across a variety of media channels, and I loved it! Most importantly, it gave me the opportunity to expand my professional network and to collaborate with many of the largest financial services and digital economy corporations in the world.

It also gave me a platform to influence the adoption of best FCC/FCR practices down the market onto regional banks, community banks, and federal credit unions that needed to fortify their FCC/FCR programs. I was able to expand the scope of FCC/FCR practices across other segments of the market, such as into the Real Estate, Digital Economy, and Business Risk Management segments, hence creating opportunities to position FCC products into those segments.

In 2016 when a U.K. headhunter approached me upon a recommendation from a very good friend from Citi, I was not actually in the market; I was not seeking job opportunities outside. I was legitimately happy and satisfied with my role in LNRS. Yes, it was not ideal, but what is ideal? Leadership was tough, and goals were ambitious. There was a great deal of challenges in that role, but it was interesting, and it was rewarding to see the results.

Question 11: "What failures have you learned from the most that have contributed to your career success?"

However, one of the dreams on my bucket list was to work and live in London. The U.K. role with HSBC gave me the right opportunity at the right time to scratch this goal out of my bucket list. This role has been very fulfilling and is allowing me to continue learning and refining my skill set through adding other disciplines under my belts, such as Surveillance and Regulatory Conduct Analytics. Thanks to this role, I now have a better understanding of model risk management and how to properly use new technologies to address business needs. I am now engaged in transformational initiatives to enhance the FCC/FCR Analytics programs across the board. None of these would be possible without the amazing support and collaboration of my team members, our leadership team, and our colleagues across other functions.

In summary, the message is that the collective effort will always reap better and more rewarding results than trying to do everything by yourself. So, even if you are pressed to deliver, make a conscious effort to share your knowledge and experience with others to up-skill your overall team. Avoid hoarding knowledge at all costs. When recruiting, do not be afraid of targeting resources that may be more qualified or more experienced than yourself; you may learn a lot from them. Maintain a continuous list of potential candidates that may be good fits for current and upcoming roles in your team or for other teams and keep in touch with them, you never know when you may need to call them in or when they may call you out for collaborative efforts like this book or for the next endeavor in your career."

WILL BROWN: "All failures bring the chance to move you forward as long as you have the ability to reflect upon the situation that led to them and then implement the changes needed to face these situations more effectively in the future.

Personally, my main early failures were in the inability to measure my aptitude for certain roles or engagements, particularly in terms of weighing up what I would need to do to be effective in a new role. Earlier in my career, I was slightly naïve (as all younger people are) about my capability to do certain roles.

Ultimately this was a good thing as I was able to learn to balance my confidence in pushing forward and accepting internal positions with a proper understanding of the skill-gaps I needed to fill to become truly successful.

The ability to be able to thoughtfully assess your own capabilities and abilities in light of what is needed in a role is crucial. Just as is assessing whether the culture exists to support you to perform these duties. You should always strive for roles that will stretch you both personally and professionally to maintain an upwards trajectory in your career. This upwards trajectory doesn't always have to be focused on a tangible outcome such as title or salary. It could be focused on what skill set you can develop to ultimately help you further your career in the future.

There is a lot about these failures that can be applied from both a professional and personal level. It's one of the aspects I enjoy most about the role that I do as most professionals I speak within the Financial Crime Compliance space see this profession as a calling instead of just another job. It allows them to reflect and move forward from failures on a professional level and implement them in their personal lives also. We've seen this with multiple showcases of individuals and banks supporting causes as a result of the work that they do.

One example is the Mansion House declaration, where over 30 Financial Institutions signed a declaration to commit to "contributing to the global fight against IWT (Illegal Wildlife Trade)." This being among the top five most lucrative global financial crime but is also a very important ecological and positive step with ramifications far outside a traditional banking role. This has meant that FCC professionals are able to link their professional focus with CSR/Ethics activities with their personal focus on improving aspects of the world, in this case, the illegal wildlife trade."

REFLECTION

How can you apply these lessons and insights to your career or life today?

_____

_____

_____

_____

_____

_____

_____

_____

_____

_____

_____

_____

When you hear the term 'career success', what/who comes to mind?
What are your top
3 tips for
career success?

QUESTION 12

TADEO (JUN) CLARAVALL: "There is a great Japanese philosophy called Ikigai, which, when I first read about it a decade ago, helped clarify in my mind what true success means for my career and my life in general.

In summary, Ikigai states, and I'm paraphrasing, that to be truly happy and successful in any endeavor, you need to find and stay at the intersection of four areas, namely, what you love to do, what you are good at, what the world needs, and what you can get paid for.

I guess I'm pretty lucky in that I was able to find my Ikigai in financial crime risk and compliance relatively early in my career and, as a result, have what I think is a productive, meaningful, and successful career.

Other people that come to mind that have found their Ikigai and I would therefore deem successful are my parents, who both reached the pinnacle of their respective careers in academia and the military. Mother Teresa, whose impact on the world, especially the poor and helpless, was unquestionable and incomparable. Abraham Lincoln, arguably the best president the United States of America has ever had.

My top tips for career success. Here's what has worked for me. Try it and see if it works for you.

1. Know what you want and why you want it. The former is the goal (e.g., role, title, company, location, comp level), and the latter is the rocket fuel that will propel you towards the goal.

2. Take massive, consistent, and intelligent action towards your goal. Action has been a cure-all for me. Anytime I feel doubt, fear, or hesitation, it's a sign that I'm stuck in my head and overthinking things. But when I take action, almost as if by magic, my doubts turn into confidence, my fears turn into courage, and my hesitation turns into positive momentum most of the time.

3. Iterate, adjust, course-correct until you reach your goal. Some actions we take turn out to be the wrong ones. But the decision to

take action seldom is. When we act, we make mistakes, and we encounter temporary defeats. No problem. That should be expected. The road to success is never a straight line. So, reflect on what happened and learn the lesson it has to offer you. Then get up, dust yourself off, and try again, do something different until you get the outcome you want.

When you reach your goal, set another one. Then rinse and repeat steps 1, 2, and 3."

JOHN CUSACK: "How about having ridden the roller coaster and got to walk away in one piece, with your professional reputation intact, and you can sleep at night! Most senior compliance leaders are eventually displaced due to an incident on their watch, which in most cases is incredibly unfair. Many of these have been the best our industry has produced, dedicated their professional careers to doing the right thing, and many were my Peers. Their careers were all successes until they weren't. For me, they remain, in many cases, still successful, and it frustrates me that this knowledge and experience is not being utilized enough. Career success can only be truly evaluated by your Peers; in other words, those who walked among you and wore your shoes know what it's like. Other opinions may have more bearing on your prospects and on what people say at the water cooler, but that must be parked and differentiated."

MARTA LIA REQUEIJO: "Be passionate about what you do. Share your knowledge. Work collaboratively."

MATT FRIEDMAN: "There are three core values I live by related to my career. First, it is essential to me that I have a job that I enjoy. Since most people spend a significant amount of time working, if we are not happy with our job, this can be a great source of anguish. Before I accept a job, I first get to know who my boss and team will be and then make the decision based on whether I think it will be the right fit. Second, for me, it is not about the money, it is about the work I will be doing. I know of many people who have great-paying jobs, but they are hopelessly unhappy. What is the use of this money if your life is not fulfilling? Finally, I accept the fact that I will be a student forever. There is never a point when we should stop learning. For this reason, I often tell people I don't want to be called an expert. It assumes I know everything that I need to know. This is often not the case."

MARTIN JAMES WALLIS: "I think career success isn't static. What you want in your teens is different from your 20s, 30s, etc.

1. What is your Goal? The more you can define what you want, the easier it is to ask for help and get guidance on how to achieve it. That takes some investigation and reflection to achieve. This can be your end goal, and then trace back the path from how others have achieved it, they will likely be very different, but often there are common themes. Remember that your goals can change, so review and revise as you develop.

2. Continual learning and development can be a challenge in finding the right resources in the information age. Still, if you have mapped out number 1, it should lead you to where you should be looking to equip yourself with the right level of understanding and skills. The internet has brought an abundance of free materials, and organizations such as the UNODC provide free training to get you started. But you may also want to think of gaining footholds in other cross-functional disciplines, coding, data analysis, and other tech-related areas.

3. Building your network, probably the most important, will help you understand the opportunities out there. The more people you can share a good chat with over coffee, virtual or otherwise, the more opportunities you will have to gain insights from those that have already been in your exact position. Again, I have found the best way is just to ask but be prepared that not everyone will want to talk and that it is nothing personal; we all have roles to fulfill."

NICK TURNER: "Personal achievement is personal. If it means being visible or leading a team, that's great. If it means leaving time for family, friends, and hobbies, that's also great.

My suggestion would be to think about what fulfillment is, commit to it, and accept that it might change over time. Whatever success is, it can't be measured in overtime or dollars."

MEL GEORGIE B. RACELA: "Each one has their own measure of career success. It is not necessarily becoming the CEO or the President. We all have diverse capabilities in varying degrees, after all. We cannot always be the tallest trees in the forest because some of us may not even be trees and by no means less important. Career success may simply mean being the best you can be in your chosen field of work. And in that journey so far, I have found the following to hold true:

First, put in the time and the effort. Success comes at a price, more often than not, in the currency of hard work.

But know when to take a break and focus on other things that matter, such as family and friends. Because it is their love and support that help make it easier for us to do our jobs.

Second, I am fortunate that the BSP has instilled in me the core values of Excellence, Integrity, Accountability, Patriotism, and Solidarity. These are the same core values that we apply in the fight against financial crimes.

And finally, learn from mistakes—mine and others. Doing so ultimately cultivates a disposition toward effectiveness and efficiency."

WILL BROWN: "I think the term career success is so subjective as it intersects so heavily with people's personal lives given the amount of time we spend on our careers. Everyone has their own perception of what is important to them and what success looks like.

As an overall point, I would define a career as a success if you have a clear mission and you're able to execute on this in a productive and rewarding way.

My first tip would be to identify what you personally want from a career. This could be as quantifiable as a specific title, salary, working in a certain location, or for a certain company. However, it could be the focus on the mission of your work or the work-life balance that you would want to have to ensure you have enough personal time to focus on other pursuits. I often speak to individuals who are set on becoming a Chief Compliance Officer, and it is almost irrelevant what company this is for. Again, this is a personal aim for the individual, but it's often important to note the culture in the company, as previously discussed.

Your career ambitions will likely change every 4 to 5 years as your personal and career life evolves. So, you should engage in a continuous activity of questioning yourself and making sure you are working towards a career that you find rewarding. However, it's important to keep focused on your overarching goals to avoid being thrown off-course, particularly during challenging times, which can test your resolve.

My second tip would be to take a long-term view on career success. It should be something that you strive for on a daily basis but also keep in your long view so that you know what you're working towards. Everyone has setbacks and will have experienced the highs and lows of working life but maintaining a more long-term focus will allow you to smooth out the edges on these highs and lows. Jun Claravall, the author of this book, is someone that I think has embodied this. He has managed to build his career aggregating the skillsets needed to be a successful Regional Head of FCC by spending time in each discipline, from AML to Sanctions, in a very deliberate fashion. At the same time, he has been able to develop people that would ultimately help him build functions effectively from job to job.

The third tip would be to enjoy the journey. It sounds very simple and clichéd, but it can be very hard to keep this in perspective. Focus on the parts of the job that you really enjoy and try to find the reward in the challenging moments, and it will allow you to enjoy success as it comes. It's often not meeting or exceeding the goal but the journey that can be most rewarding. Sports people often articulate this in the myriad different autobiographies out there - the reward is often in the struggle."

JOHN FOGARTY: "Three things:

1. Being a good people manager. You are only as good as your team in this environment, and the stronger the team around you, the better the results.

2. Be humble and respectful. Admit your failures and learn from them – but never do them again!

3. Celebrate success as a team.

JEROME MICHAILIDIS: "One thing comes to mind – being excited to go to work. If you dread going to work every day, I don't think you are truly successful."

JESSICA HODSON: "Career success, I always think a good way to see it is if someone has joy in their life. Some people don't love their job, and that's fine. Even if you don't love your job, but you find joy in your life, that is success to me.

My top 3 tips are:

1. Growth mindset. Try and keep reviewing your skillset, ability, and knowledge as an ever-evolving beast. Ask for internal secondments, take lateral moves for roles that build upon your weaknesses, and ask to spend time with those who are better than you in certain areas. Financial Crime Compliance will always have new trends, new problems to solve, and new roles coming up. Staying stagnant and too self-assured in your ability can become people's undoing.

2. Never overestimate your talent and forget the hard work and luck which got you (or your idol) to where they are. I think a lot of the time, it is easy to look at people who are successful or to look at our own success with talent-tinted glasses. Find that inner drive and motivator and never forget it. It won't be your talent to get you to where you want to go.

3. Be curious. There are SO many free financial crime talks, forums, podcasts, groups, etc., which are a treasure trove of information (also great for networking!). Sometimes the application of financial crime legislation can be quite subjective depending on which firm you work for, so ask people, talk to peers. Almost all of the MLRO's I know are part of sector groups, peer roundtables, or have WhatsApp groups! None assume they know it all, and every single one of them relies on a peer group for information and to ask curious questions to."

MAGGIE QIU: "Doing well in what you love.

The three tips I have: 1) Find what you love to do; 2) do things that leverage your strengths, and 3) have the continuing passion for keeping doing it."

ARMINA ANTONIOU: "Have an open mind – whether this is in respect of your career path or how you work to solve problems faced in your current role, having an open mind will allow you to embrace all opportunities and think as flexibly as the highly motivated and agile criminals that we seek to detect and disrupt.

As someone with a law degree, it was very easy to continue a career in law. That was a logical and well-trodden path. But I knew that my training and approach to solving problems could be applied in multiple fields, and (while it took me a while to make the career change), this mindset allowed me to pivot from a career in the law to a career in Risk.

Now that I work in FinCrime, I have found that the regulations, guidance, and advice in the Financial Crime Prevention area were largely written with the banks in mind. When I started my role, most guidance was targeted to financial services, and the limited gambling-related guidance (published by various regulators and FATF) was aimed at Casino based gambling. Working in a racing and sports betting environment, none of this Casino based guidance was directly relevant. However, understanding the similarities across industries and seeking to understand the criminal behavior being found, my team considers how similar criminal behavior or similar compliance strategies might be used in our industry to achieve the objectives of detecting and disrupting financial crimes.

2. Be passionate – being passionate about what you do is essential to having the drive to excelling in a challenging field. For me, I am passionate about what I do because I know that my role makes it a little harder for criminals to operate freely. And this, in turn, keeps society safe from crimes affecting the vulnerable, crimes involving drugs, terrorist activities, and corruption.

3. Be persistent, determined, and confident in your own skills … show your Grit. I have always been a fan of stories about underdogs overcoming the odds. Hearing about how people from backgrounds absent of privilege, with limited or difficult access to education, resources, or networks of people have been able to succeed in their chosen field in the face of those challenges. The real-life stories of footballers like Marta, Pele, and Australian national team player Hayley Raso or the background of Australian Formula 1 drivers Alan Jones and Mark Webber are inspirational to me – these are people who overcame structural, financial, or physical challenges which would have stopped ordinary people in their tracks. These people have all found success in their fields despite those challenges.

I have found that Grit and determination were necessary for me to endure the professional challenges that working in Financial Crime has thrown at me. I didn't start my career as a risk professional, took on a role at a difficult time during litigation brought by a regulator but was nonetheless able to push through all those challenges and build out a new financial crime risk framework despite that. I did this because I believed that I could make a difference in disrupting criminal activity, and I was very determined to prove that.

The research of psychologist, author, and amazing TEDTalk-er Angela Duckworth has since tied this together for me – Duckworth found that Grit was highly predictive of success in students, more so than IQ. Grit, according to Duckworth, is passion and sustained persistence towards long-term achievement, with no particular concern for recognition or rewards."

SCOTT BURTON: "Someone who really enjoys their job is my definition of career success. Having a "can do" and helpful attitude, be patient and display perseverance and have attention to details."

ABTAR RANDHAWA: "Success has a committed team who feel that work is not an obligation but a meaningful task with a measurable success factor. This does not always have to manifest itself through remuneration but also recognition for the contribution and efforts made. Being continually acknowledged and respected are critical for recognizing overall career success as well as providing much-needed motivational boosts in this ever challenging and complex organizational environment we operate in."

JAIKUMAR (JAI) RAMASWAMY: "There are several ways to measure career success: compensation, position, and contribution. I have always measured success less by compensation and stature than by contribution. To me, the biggest marker of success is to make the world a little bit better. The three tips I would give are: (1) find an organization with a mission that you find compelling; (2) try always to be challenged in whatever work you do; and (3) make sure that you are comfortable with the organizational culture. In my experience, these three things are far better determinations of career success than money or titles."

ANTHONY NAPPI: "Career success is dependent on the person; what is success for one person may not be considered a success for another. However, for me, it was building a team of professionals who were treated with respect, who were able to move from being professional colleagues to being friends – people who cared about one another, who felt valued and were able to have a work-life balance.

Question 12: "When you hear the term 'career success', what/who comes to mind? What are your top 3 tips for career success?"

157

Have a career roadmap so that you know the destination you want to achieve.

Be willing to take chances and know that every move does not need to be a promotion – you will need to take some lateral moves in order to move up.

Have balance and perspective and a strong moral compass (integrity, honesty, compassion, empathy, courage)."

CARLOS GARCIA PAVIA: "Career success is very subjective; it absolutely depends on what your priorities in life are. Some may think that going up to the top of the ladder is a success; however, it may have an undesirable cost for your life/work balance. Through the years, I have repeatedly heard many folks saying: "of course, being a highly compensated C-level executive with a robust golden parachute must make life a dream." Personally, I disagree with such a view as I am well aware of the legal and regulatory obligations that, if breached, may rapidly terminate the path of apparently successful careers. We all have seen multiple cases of CEOs, CFOs, and others that have collapsed in disgrace.

In my very personal view, career success is defined by doing what you are passionate to do, doing what you enjoy doing, and influencing others to share your vision. Compensation is important, but I would suggest not to make it your main driver. Otherwise, you may end up jumping from role to role and likely from organization to organization in pursuit of the next few dollars but not achieving actual fulfillment in your career.

Have you heard about the "rat race"? have you seen a hamster running tirelessly into its spinning wheel going nowhere? Do not sabotage your career by pursuing the elusive dollar figure; that is a dangerous trap and one that may enslave you for life. Once you reach your target dollar figure, you will be pursuing the next, and then the next, and so on. You get the idea, and it is a never-ending race, a race fueled by greed.

Instead of enrolling yourself in the rat race, be very disciplined with your finances from the start of your career by following these basic principles:

Learn to live within your means.

Learn to save consistently. From day one of your career, you must start saving for retirement. Do not postpone this unless you must.

From the early stages of your career, educate yourself about retirement. Do not misunderstand retirement as an age or a time when you must depart from the working force. Retirement is rather the time when you can finally focus on the things that you want to do, rather than doing the things that you have to do. Wouldn't it be better to be in a position to do what you want to do at an early age in your life rather than waiting for your older years just to realize that you may not be able to do those things anymore?

At all costs, avoid acquiring and accumulating debt.

Avoid withdrawing or lending money from your retirement fund.

Do not get things that you want if you cannot afford to pay for them in cash. If you want that, save for it first.

Do not be greedy in your approach to invest. Understand the risk and make well-educated decisions; otherwise, you may face significant losses. As we all have heard repeatedly, if it seems too good to be true, it most likely is.

Focus on building up your net-worth, not your credit score.

I would have loved receiving these recommendations when I started my career. It would have positioned me to likely be in a comfortable place to enjoy retirement at this point in my life. This is not a complaint but a reflection of how the lack of knowledge of these basic principles may push you away from feeling that sense of success in your career. Bottom line, I believe that career success is the fulfillment of your personal goals through the fruits of your hard work, while establishing a legacy that will outlive you."

GUILLERMO HORTA: "To work on something that you passionately live and breathe, to feel recognized for the added value you bring to your employer and to walk back home on a daily basis knowing you have been doing the right thing to help the world. A Financial Crimefighter should have the three ingredients of leadership: direction, alignment and commitment."

ERIC FAVILA: "This has been a difficult question for me for a long time. Personally, I have struggled to define what it is. More importantly, what is it for me? I felt that in the corporate world it is compensation and status. These things are quite nice, but in many cases, it is a conflict with what makes us happy and eats into our well-being.

What I have come to understand is that 'career success' is about balancing our individuality with how we interact with the world. This means taking the time and energy to get to know ourselves. What motivates and burns us out? What makes us happy, sad, and angry? There is no career out there that delivers only one aspect. However, knowing who you gives clarity to the career options we have in life. Being a financial crime fighter isn't the most financially rewarding profession out there. It is probably one of the most frustrating and depressing jobs. It is thankless. In many corporate environments, I have observed, it is hard for compliance professionals are not that popular among organizations. In the most difficult of times, we get exposed to the worst of humanity that law enforcement regularly sees.

I've always admired people who appear to have figured out their purpose. Regardless of what they did, they looked successful. Those in pursuit of their purpose are probably asking the obvious question – what is my purpose? Maybe what is missing is a strong relationship with the self. Understanding the self. Instead of looking outwards seeking careers that deliver money, status, or some other altruistic benefit, look inwards. When we know ourselves deeply and intensely, we will gravitate to the appropriate careers. And it doesn't matter what these careers are. Street-food seller or bank CEO, it is hard to be successful in any career if it does not balance with who we are.

Success comes from within. What we do for a living is the observable manifestation of this."

How can you apply these lessons and insights to your career or life today?

_____

_____

_____

_____

_____

_____

_____

_____

_____

_____

_____

_____

_____

Was there ever a time when you
wished you took a
different career path?
Why did you decide to stay in/
return to
financial crime?

QUESTION 13

TADEO (JUN) CLARAVALL: "Honestly, no, not once have I wished I took a different career.

I think it's because I feel a deep sense of mission and pride whenever I answer people's questions about 'what I do'. A financial trader might say he trades stocks. An investment banker might say she helps raise money for companies, I on the other hand (and I did this on a couple of occasions), would grab a newspaper or point to a T.V. news channel covering news of corruption, drug-related crimes, terrorism, and say, I help prevent bad things like this from happening. Nothing wrong with being a trader or a banker. They serve a need in the market. But I'm just not sure that if I embarked on those careers that I would feel as good as I feel now with how I'm spending my life energy every day.

And one more thing, the people that work in anti-financial crimes are some of the kindest, generous, self-sacrificing, and overall good people that you'll find. Sure, there are exceptions, but a vast majority are people that you would invite over to dinner with your family or people that you would not hesitate to have your child work for in the future. That is saying a lot!"

GUILLERMO HORTA: "No, never. I always dreamed of being a politician, but never liked the dirty environment, therefore here I am, on the other side of the equation but equally working on something to live in a better place."

JOHN FOGARTY: "I had that chance earlier in my career, moving from Policing to Compliance, albeit always in a profession that satisfied that core sense of purpose of trying to do what's right."

MATT FRIEDMAN: "Years ago, I was invited to do public health checks for the Indian government within the red-light districts. I had a police officer accompany me. At one of the brothels, upon entering the waiting area, an 11-year-old Nepalese trafficking victim saw me and ran

Question 13: "Was there ever a time when you wished you took a different career path? Why did you decide to stay in/ return to financial crime?"

163

up to me. She wrapped her arms around my waist, and in Nepalese she said, "Save me, save me, they are doing terrible things to me!"

I looked down in shock at this young girl. She had straight black hair cut in a simple hanging style that reached to her shoulders. A dress, ten sizes too big, hung on her small frame. She had a pre-adolescent body. This was a child in an adult world. I can never forget the pleading desperation in her light brown eyes.

I turned to the police officer and said, "We need to take this girl out of here now."

"No, we can't do that," he said.

"Why not? You're a cop!"

"Because they will kill us before they will let us leave with her. Finding a child this age will create a lot of problems for them."

We left, frustrated, but returned several hours later with more police officers. When we arrived back, the young girl was gone. While the officers did a thorough job searching every floor, she was never found.

I will never know what happened to that precious child, but I am sure it included beatings, torture, and a drastically shortened life full of misery.

Every once in a while, each of us is given a life test. This was mine, and I failed. I should have found a way to get that girl out of that awful place, and I didn't.

For weeks after encountering this child, I had traumatic nightmares. I was haunted by the stricken expression etched across her face, along with those pleading eyes looking up at me. I would wake up in a cold sweat with my heart pounding in my chest. During these times, I imagined the things I could have done to help her. I could have simply picked her up and ran down the stairs. I could have had the police officer leave and come back with more officers while I stayed at the brothel. There were many other options that came to my mind. The fact that I failed to do these things weighed heavily on my heart.

Not knowing what else to do, I finally surrendered. I accepted the fact that knowing what I did about this problem, I could no longer turn away. I had to step up and become fully involved. At that moment, an activist was born. Many people who fight this injustice have a similar story to tell. The reality of the pain and suffering gets under a person's skin. Once absorbed, there is no escaping it.

Whenever I feel like changing what I do, I think about this girl. She brings me back to what is important in life. This is why I stay."

JESSICA HODSON: "Luckily for me, I have been in love with financial crime recruitment since I started, perhaps aside from the sometimes-wistful thought of moving into a financial crime advisory role! I have a huge passion and love for financial crime recruitment, and I know how lucky I am to work in a space I love."

JEROME MICHAILIDIS: "Many times. Consider how I fell into this world. But the stability of this lifestyle has kept me in."

MEL GEORGIE B. RACELA: "Prior to becoming the Executive Director of the AMLC Secretariat in 2017, I've held positions in the BSP for 21 years in the areas of banking supervision, legal counseling, and litigation as well as financial investigation. In retrospect, every single post prepared me for what I do now. It may have been an unconscious decision, but everything eventually fell into place."

CARLOS GARCIA PAVIA: "No, I have not experienced such a wish yet. However, I really enjoy cooking and baking. So, I would probably have traded my career in F.C. to pursue a career in the culinary industry. I have always dreamed of running my own fine cuisine Mexican restaurant. I have been very disappointed with some of the so-called Mexican restaurants that I have visited around the world, only to realize that they are misrepresenting what Mexican cuisine actually is. As I always say when asked about the best Mexican food in the area: "come to my house and see."

For those that are curious, not all Mexican food is spicy. You want real spicy food, try Indian, Thai, and even Jamaican food. Mexican food is much more than tacos and quesadillas. Each region of Mexico offers a wide variety of unique textures, flavors, colors, aromas, and sounds for the enjoyment of all senses. I am passionate about our authentic Mexican cuisine, and few are the restaurants out of Mexican borders that can actually boast about having an authentic fine Mexican cuisine offering. I invite you to visit Mexico City if you want to experience a good variety of the food from different regions of Mexico."

Question 13: "Was there ever a time when you wished you took a different career path? Why did you decide to stay in/ return to financial crime?"

165

JOHN CUSACK: "No. I was offered several senior front-line roles over the years. Still, I preferred to remain a subject matter expert, albeit over a vast and expanding subject matter, then a subject matter enthusiast. I suspect the roles I was offered were essentially high risk from a compliance perspective so that it might have felt like a busman's holiday. Still, perhaps that's a lack of ambition or risk-taking. Alternatively, it could have been avoiding poisoned chalices."

PAUL (PADDY) O'HARA: "No, but I wish I'd studied law at university; it would have really helped."

How can you apply these lessons and insights to your career or life today?

_____

_____

_____

_____

_____

_____

_____

_____

_____

_____

_____

_____

How do you feel about
mentoring?
Do you believe that it can help
in developing a financial crime
fighter's career? Are there any
mentoring stories that you can
share?

QUESTION 14

TADEO (JUN) CLARAVALL: "I'm a huge advocate of mentoring, and question 14 reminds me of this quote.

"Don't be ashamed to need help. Like a soldier storming a wall, you have a mission to accomplish. And if you've been wounded and you need a comrade to pull you up? So what?" –Marcus Aurelius, Roman emperor and Stoic philosopher

There is no doubt in my mind that I would not have been able to do all that I have done in my career without the help of a few good mentors. Mentors who helped me with my weaknesses and blind spots, mentors who helped me when I got stuck with a problem I have never had to face before, mentors who helped me keep moving forward and stopped me from self-destructing at times.

What makes for a good mentor? A good mentor will tell you what worked in their career, but they will not insist that you do it their way.

A good mentor guides you to a new and better approach when thinking about your problem or situation. A good mentor who offers excellent advice understands that their goal is to help you on your unique journey.

Here are my three tips for finding good mentors.

First, pick three people with skills you need, the experience you lack, relationships you can leverage, and perspectives you can trust. These tend to be the leaders, innovators, and talented people in our field.

Second, consider which mentors can be trusted to give you good advice and valuable information when you need it.

Third, pick a mentor who is willing to ask you tough questions and someone you are willing to be unconditionally open to about the truth. There is a place for cheerleading, which is helpful at times, but what creates lasting change are uncomfortable conversations that get into the heart of your fears and insecurities. Therefore, for the relationship to work, you and your mentor need to have an earnest desire, to be honest, learn, grow and be open to new directions.

Question 14: "Was there ever a time when you wished you took a different career path? Why did you decide to stay in/ return to financial crime?"

169

Having a mentor is fulfilling and worthwhile. They did far more than help me get ahead in my career. They helped me create a blueprint, a map for how to navigate my life more generally. They helped me through difficult situations that I would have otherwise been utterly incapable of navigating successfully on my own. They helped forge me into the person, the professional, the leader that I am today."

PATRICIA SULLIVAN: "I am a big fan of mentoring, but I came to it organically. I have benefitted from a couple of mentors who went out of their way for me, but it wasn't through a formal mentor program. I mentioned above that I took my first FCC job in 2007. Within days of arriving in this new team, the Global Head of the program and America's head of the program moved on from their positions setting off a significant FCC leadership transition and period of instability.

A senior leader from overseas was seconded to our team for a couple of months to help stabilize during this transition. It is only due to the guidance and support I received from this amazing and inspirational leader that I subsequently became the Americas Head. He helped build my confidence in my FCC knowledge and leadership skills, and that made all the difference. Other key and brilliant mentors shaped and nurtured how I think about fighting financial crime and influencing change internally and externally. I am eternally grateful to them and have paid it forward. Over the years, there have been many individuals I have taken 'under my wing' and mentored in different ways. It is a part of leadership I really enjoy, and it extends even when the job has ended.

Of great surprise and joy to me is how some of these mentees in turn 'mentored' me back in ways unexpected but so valuable. We all have different strengths, so I now look at all mentoring as a two-way street."

JOHN CUSACK: "I have benefited from mentoring from the start of my career throughout and still today, and I have tried to pay this back throughout my career. These are all personal relationships, and these work best, but organized mentoring can work too. No one is the finished article, no one really knows what they are doing at first, and role models and mentors make the difference, as each new challenge presents itself."

LUCY MASTERS: "I am a strong believer in mentoring and have personally benefited from wonderful mentors at all stages of my career who have always provided me with great encouragement, inspiration, and guidance. The most valuable piece of advice I have received regarding my leadership (and self-leadership) is to be authentic and be very aware of the shadow you are casting and the legacy you are leaving. Accordingly, I have always tried to lead authentically and by example and not expect anyone in my team to do anything I would not ask of myself. This approach has rewarded me with very motivated, engaged, and loyal team members over my career to date, and I have gained many valuable friendships that have lasted and lasted way past the end of an actual role or assignment."

MARTA LIA REQUEIJO: "Success today is having the ability to navigate challenges and being able to make the right choices for the situation at hand. This is where a mentor can be essential.

The key value of the mentor is knowledge and experience of the organization or context where the mentee is seeking support. The mentor has a 'been there and done that' input that is of extreme value when one is posed with a new challenge. The mentor shares knowledge and life experiences and helps the mentee become what they aspire to be.

I have been fortunate to have been inspired by great mentors, and I would not be where I am today without them. When I first managed a team, I was mentored by a very experienced manager; when I got back to work from maternity leave, I had the support of a very senior woman in a leadership role, and when I worked in one Tier 1 bank, a seasoned director helped me navigate the very complex matrix environment.

Mentoring is a two-way street – both mentor and mentee will grow with the experience. As a mentor, it is incredibly fulfilling to be able to help someone else unlock their potential. It is also a great way to be introduced to new perspectives."

MAGGIE QIU: "Mentoring is essential. They can be the role models you learned from, you can be your cheerleaders, and they can be your career coach and even a life coach.

My mentors have helped me in developing my career in FCC. After being rejected by my dream company, I was so disappointed and mad at myself for not doing enough. My mentor Deborah told me, "There will always be good opportunities, no need to feel sorry for not getting this one, but rather view this as a learning opportunity to reflect on what you can do better next time." Her encouragement had a profound impact on

Question 14: "Was there ever a time when you wished you took a different career path? Why did you decide to stay in/ return to financial crime?"

171

my career, and I think about this every time I fail or experience rejection."

MATT FRIEDMAN: "Mentoring is an essential part of our learning. During my four-decade career, I have been blessed with great mentors. Much of the benefit I gained from these enlightened people was derived from their personal stories. What sometimes surprised me was that while some of those stories initially seemed irrelevant, later in my life they became influential.

One of my most significant mentors told me that he had decided to work with me because he felt he had something to offer. However, he went on to say: "This is a gift I offer to you. But once you have achieved a similar status in your life, you need to pass this gift on to others. We must all repay the kindness. It is not something to be consumed – it is something to be shared and recycled. Promise me you will accept the fact that if we receive, we must also give back." Thus, I consider being a mentor is an honor, a privilege, and a responsibility."

MARTIN JAMES WALLIS: "Over the years, I have had some great mentors, and I have also had the opportunity to be considered a mentor. Whether this is formal or informal, I think there is a prevailing collaborative and cooperative mindset within the anti-financial crime community by the shared vision. I am still on that journey and look to experienced individuals within the financial crime field and in business that I respect and try to draw on their experiences to help me understand how I can achieve more or be better at what I am trying to do. I like to think that in those conversations, I can also give back; as for me, I see it as very much a two-way street. Sometimes that one conversation can unlock a whole pathway.

I was also very humbled by the support I was given as I transitioned out of the military into the corporate world. I was fortunate that with one large bank, I had several calls with the AML team, all the way to their global head in Hong Kong, who took over an hour of his time to talk through where my skills could be used in financial crime and what roles were available. I am very thankful for the insights I received."

JESSICA HODSON: "Yes without question, I think that mentoring can make a huge difference. Not only for the knowledge, life skills and abilities it teaches the person, but also the doors it opens.

I very recently had someone interviewing for a role within another bank, and by coincidence her former mentor from her graduate years (5+ years ago), was now in the New York office, saw her name on the interview sheet and she got the job!

Stories like these give me pause as I reflect on how important networks for minority groups and how hard they can be to infiltrate.

As alluded to above, networks and "who you know" is sometimes the defining factor of if someone gets a job. People who are of minority or of lower socio-economic backgrounds don't often have exposure to these networks and opportunities. Mentoring is a small but effective way to branch out into these area's and bridge the gap, albeit in a small way."

ANTHONY NAPPI: "Being part of a mentor-mentee relationship is a great way to grow in your career by listening to, sharing with someone whom you trust and can help you develop in your career. Mentoring can help anyone as long as you have a good mentor whom you trust, you define a clear and specific objective you want to achieve, you invest in your own development, and you come to the mentoring sessions with an open mind.

I had the opportunity to have a mentor; he was a world-class professional, someone I trusted implicitly and who provided me with the opportunity to speak openly and freely and provided excellent suggestions for how I could improve in my career. He was great at listening and asking questions. I truly benefited from this experience and used much of what he taught me in mentoring sessions with the many people I have and continue to mentor."

PAUL (PADDY) O'HARA: "Mentoring or coaching helps everyone, but only if you have a specific issue that you need help getting clear in your head. Then it's really powerful. The rapport you have with a mentor could end up being a lifetime association but should start out issue-specific."

MEL GEORGIE B. RACELA: "In anything, having a mentor is a bonus; not everyone gets to have one. Some are thrown in the deep end, and it is sink or swim. Guidance from a mentor hopefully provides for a steeper learning curve. Often, mentors also make for good examples. When it is time to take the helm, you'll find yourself emulating a pastiche of superiors from whom you've learned most.

Question 14: "Was there ever a time when you wished you took a different career path? Why did you decide to stay in/ return to financial crime?"

173

I was fortunate to have found a mentor in one of the former executive directors of the AMLC Secretariat and in one of the former BSP Governors, now deceased, Nestor A. Espenilla Jr. The first always insisted on not giving up no matter what, and the latter taught me to work hard and to always think outside the box, so here I am."

GUILLERMO HORTA: "Absolutely. I'm a total advocate for mentoring. I personally participate in different mentorship programs where I have been able to provide advice to members of my team. Mentorship not only provides direction and guidance but also encourages people to feel motivated and passionate about their work, while also gives me a sense of satisfaction of helping others to achieve their career goals."

CARLOS GARCIA PAVIA: "I am a firm believer in mentoring, not only serving as a mentor but also being a mentee. It is a rewarding experience, one that enables you to discover more of yourself and to get to know more about your strengths and your opportunities for improvement. Some say that to progress your career, you need to focus on your strengths, on what you do very well. Others advise you to focus on your opportunities for improvement, not to say weaknesses. In my view, there is no right or wrong response to this; both options may be equally valid. However, I am more inclined to focus on our weaknesses, even more on those weaknesses that we may not be self-aware of. Yes, all of us have blind spots, and while we are particularly good at identifying weaknesses in others, we are not so good at identifying those in ourselves.

Being a mentor or a mentee gives us the opportunity to learn about those blemishes in a safe and constructive environment. Mentoring is more about triggering thoughts and elaborate reflections that will lead to adjustments in our behaviors. Mentoring is not about giving or receiving guidance and direction. Mentoring is about enabling us to understand and discover ourselves better and how we can use our uniqueness to bring the best of our capabilities to support our career progression and the goals of our organizations."

SCOTT BURTON: "Mentoring is critical for fast-tracking career development. Regular catch-ups and the ability to openly discuss issues is very important. It provides an alternative viewpoint that you may not obtain from an employee and manager relationship. I would definitely recommend actively seeking out mentors (just a couple is fine), and it can be done via informal or formal channels. My experience of when it works best is when it's informal."

Question 14: "Was there ever a time when you wished you took a different career path? Why did you decide to stay in/ return to financial crime?"

175

REFLECTION

How can you apply these lessons and insights to your career or life today?

_____

_____

_____

_____

_____

_____

_____

_____

_____

_____

_____

_____

_____

What is your typical
daily schedule?
Do you have any hints
for managing
work-related stress?
How do you stay
productive?

QUESTION 15

TADEO (JUN) CLARAVALL: "Since I became an independent anti-financial crime practitioner for over two years, I typically slice my 24-hour day into three parts (these are averages that I try to hit as consistently as possible). Eight hours of focused work. Eight hours of sleep, rest, and recovery. Eight hours for everything else that is not working or sleep, rest, and recovery; this includes book writing/ reading, self-development, podcasting, relationships, recreation, exercise, errands, etc.

The advantage of working for myself is that I'm able to work when I want to work, and so long as I hit the 8 hours total on average, I'm happy. This 8-8-8 method works for me because I feel I'm living a well-rounded life as a result.

As for managing work-related stress, I have a simple three-part strategy:

First, I take care of my body and mind. Everything we do in life requires the use of our body and mind. Our body and mind require energy to operate. The fastest way to get stressed and burn out is to try and work with an energy deficit. I generate energy via restorative sleep, healthy and nutritious food, regular cardio and strength exercises, and regular meditation practice to prevent this. I also try not to do more in a day that I can recover from in a day, meaning I try not to expend energy that I cannot replenish within 24 hours. Expending more than you can replenish is like spending more money than what you earn. There will be reckoning that is going to happen at some point. The deficit will need to be paid back somehow in disease or ill health, costly mistakes at work, or damaged relationships. No one wants that.

Second, I try to control my focus. I try to be as clear as possible on the outcomes that I want in any situation and focus on that outcome. This allows me to gauge what's important vs what's not, what's essential vs what's a distraction, which email to respond to, which call to pick up, which message to read, and which message to delete. Having a clear focus on your outcomes is like having a laser beam pointing to a target. There may be a million other things going on around simultaneously, but the laser goes straight to its target and cuts through any obstacle put on its way.

The third is controlling my mindset. I try to find the good in everything, the positive meaning of events, and the positive intentions of other people's actions. I believe nature is neutral. It is people that assign positive or negative connotations to events. People's actions and intentions are, in my experience, generally good. Sure, some people are out to cheat you or take unfair advantage of you and have other bad intentions, but those are in the tiny minority in my experience. So why would I suffer the angst and anxiety of thinking negatively about people's actions when 9.9 times out of 10 it is not warranted? For the times when someone's bad actions blindside me, I reflect on it, learn not to be blindsided again, then move on. In this game, I'm willing to play the odds so that I can work and live with a positive mindset and enjoy the experience.

My best productivity tips.

I've been a student of productivity for as early as I can remember. My belief is that time is our most precious resource. Therefore, making sure that we use our time wisely to pursue what's most important to us is what I think being productive is all about.

Top tips:

1. Goal clarity - for me, the primary way I gauge productivity is whether I am effectively using my time and energy to make progress towards a goal that I've decided is important to me. So, it all starts with the goal, the target. You may be busy and active all day, but unless you can link that activity to a goal you are working towards, then that's not being productive. I call that doing busy work, and you are likely busy helping someone else reach their goals instead.

2. Protect your prime time – think about your typical day. Don't you have periods where you feel completely focused and energized? I call those periods your 'prime time. Protect them. They are one of your secret weapons to high productivity. For me, I notice I'm in the prime time zone during three periods, 8 to 10 am, 2 to 4 pm, and 7 to 9 pm. I block those times in my calendar to work on my most important and challenging tasks or conversations with people. Of course, I release those blocks if there's an important meeting, call, or crisis (important being the operative word here).

But whoever is asking for my time and attention during these periods must fight for it. If you are clear on your goals and have decided on what's important, spending your prime time on anything else doesn't make any sense.

3. Incentivize and celebrate productivity – humans thrive on incentives. Whether we do or don't take a particular action is influenced heavily by incentives. I like to practice delayed gratification most times. This means, when I set a goal or a task to complete, I hold up an incentive for me at the end if I achieve it. It can be as simple as a coffee or a walk after I finish a 90 min work sprint, or for big goals taking that trip with the family if I get that promotion. On the flip side, disincentives work too in preventing or dissuading me from becoming lazy or distracted. It can be as simple as donating money to a cause that I am opposed to if I procrastinate three times on a challenging but essential task. This has been so effective that I have yet to give a single dollar to an 'anti-charity to date. I'd instead do what I've been procrastinating on than support a group that I am deeply against."

JEROME MICHAILIDIS: "A typical day has a lot of meetings and discussions. To stay productive, one should focus on a few key things to complete each day. It is unrealistic to expect everything to be completed, so it requires prioritization."

MARTIN JAMES WALLIS: "If you search how to be more productive, you'll find various methodologies to help you focus on your tasks at hand; we all work differently and have different productive periods, so making sure you maximize your focus time in those areas is a good place to start.

My routine starts with some personal activity; I then quickly scan my messages to triage what has come in. If I have a particularly challenging task, I will hit that first for a couple of hours before the inbox. If it is a critical task, I will block out time when needed in the calendar to turn off alerts. We have a high degree of transparency and trust, so it is easy for someone to update their status to do not disturb without judgment.

Working for a global company and multiple time zones means that most weeks, there are days where it can involve working late. I try to carve out time for dinner and talk with my family before breaking back into it. You cannot be 24/7, so creating the boundaries that work for you and are also in harmony with your team or broader company are what will help sustain working over the long term and how you will remain productive in your work as well as enjoying your life."

NICK TURNER: "My days begin and end with emails because my colleagues and clients are all over the world.

Here's my big tip: Sort your emails by subject instead of date and categorize them according to the day of the week you intend to action them. My inbox is also my to-do list. When I'm done with something, I file it and forget it."

JOHN CUSACK: "Daily Schedule I'll skip as what works for me might not work for others. As for stress - that's what other people do to you, so don't compound it with putting any more on yourself. When facing stress, have a routine that works. Mine is to know you will come through it, you have in the past, and you will do again. Focus on the task, know what you can do to improve the situation, work hard, have the right team. This works every time for me. Productivity is a function of being able to prioritize and access the right experience in the time available. That means having a great contact list and great relationships and sometimes being "unproductive" by helping others on their priorities too."

ANTHONY NAPPI: "I have found that having a stress relief valve is important; for me, it was physical exercise; it was time I am able to forget about work and just work out. With that said, as I have grown in my career, I have reassessed what is most important and have come to the conclusion that my family, my health, my faith and then my job are most important – does not mean I do not work hard, but I work with balance and perspective. Put another way; I work to live and do not live to work. The time you miss with your family and friends is time you will never get back, and if it is really important, you have a lifetime to build your career."

GUILLERMO HORTA: "My schedule is terrible, probably no different than other Executives in the Financial Crime arena. I start around 8:30 am with meetings and video conferences, and calls. Due to Covid-19, my working schedule has been worst. I used to block in my calendar at least 1 hour on a daily basis for "Lunch and emails catch up", which ultimately helped me to stand up, walk for a bit during the day, etc. Now everyone

Question 15: "What is your typical daily schedule? Do you have any hints for managing work-related stress? How do you stay productive?"

181

knows you are at home, that you should be available and that there is no place to go, so meetings are longer, later, and more frequent. It is imperative to exercise and to let our mind rest for a few hours. My weeks are flying without noticing it!"

JESSICA HODSON: "Typically, my day starts with a workout as this helps me with my stress and ensures I start work "awake." More than that, though, I know sometimes I don't leave my desk, so it's important to me that I move.

The most important thing I do is triage my emails and messages. This means I go through and action all things which require my immediate attention, and others I will put into my calendar to action later or respond. Having a clear inbox, to me personally, is such a great reliever of stress and feeling pressured.

Staying productive is a tricky one, I think more so if you're having a "quiet" workday. I tend to have little projects to the side which aren't very time-sensitive, which I can switch to if work is a little quiet. I live by the theory that productivity breeds productivity, so try to stay busy to keep my momentum up.

There is a really cool theory which I heard of recently, called Parkinson's Law, you'll have to look it up for the full definition, but it's a very interesting way to view allocating your time in a day."

LUCY MASTERS: "My daily schedule is unpredictable and generally does not transpire in the way I thought it might! To ensure I deal with the most important (vs. just the urgent) tasks in any one day, I carve out some time in the early morning to set my intention on the few things that I must accomplish that day. While I do not have full control over my calendar, I schedule these commitments to myself, so they are in existence. Then, at the end of my day, I spend some time reflecting directly on the intentions I set for myself that morning. Apart from this, my greatest hint for managing work-related stress is staying focussed in the present moment at any given time."

SCOTT BURTON: "I typically try and time block tasks, e.g., emails, document reviews meetings; depending on the urgency of tasks, I take on the most difficult tasks first thing in the mornings. Working in a fast-paced and demanding industry, I try and allocate time for exercise most days. This helps keep my mind clear and reduce stress levels."

MEL GEORGIE B. RACELA: "Although we do have work-from-home arrangements, I am normally at the office, and I arrive by 8 a.m. I go through my day, reviewing documents, holding or attending meetings, responding to e-mails and messages, attending to personnel matters, among other things. My day does not usually end when I leave the office, though, as urgent matters may come up anytime—the repercussion of technology, which makes you available all the time.

The volume of the workload can be overwhelming, and the key to seeing it through is having a reliable and competent workforce. There are only so many hours in a day, so you must accept that you cannot accomplish everything alone. A well-capacitated and happy workforce, however, makes these all worthwhile."

WILL BROWN: "Typically, my daily schedule will involve a glass of water and some kind of exercise before heading to the office early to make sure I can start my day off productively and without distractions. It will involve planning my day to ensure I've set my priorities and also the teams in line with our weekly/monthly priorities.

I'm fortunate to be something of an early riser. That allows me time for a morning routine before the rest of my daily priorities' takeover. I'll typically be at my desk around 7 – 7:30 am; the flip side of this is that I'm in bed nice and early! Typically, I am less productive in the evenings, so I focus my day around knowing when I'm most active and engaged.

This also allows me to engage with candidates and clients early in the morning as I will typically have to be available around their busy schedules to make sure we can have a productive conversation before they start their day.

Knowing myself and when I'm most productive at certain times allows me to be able to maximize when I'm going to best at certain activities. This means that I'll typically schedule administrative activities for just after lunch so that the more procedural part of my day-to-day work can be completed, and I save my creativity for when I am feeling energized!

An inevitable part of everyone's jobs is that there will be some element of work-related stress. I've typically found it very useful to schedule routine activities that can elevate some of this stress. These would normally take the form of playing some sport – rugby/golf or going to the gym. Then also spending time away from work either with friends or family to get perspective.

Question 15: "What is your typical daily schedule? Do you have any hints for managing work-related stress? How do you stay productive?"

These are habits I started very early on in my life, even before I commenced my career. Rugby, in particular, is a very effective form of stress relief!

For more immediate relief, I find it always useful to take a step back from a situation and speak to people that I work with or, sometimes even more usefully, get additional viewpoints from an external perspective. This allows me to frame things that are happening in a wider context rather than react to the immediate. Perspective is always useful when really looking to see how urgent something truly is and to try to keep the negative in perspective. It is often never as bad as it seems in the moment!"

PAUL (PADDY) O'HARA: "Life is tough at the moment, holding down two roles, so it's 12 hours of meetings, with a couple of hours of email time at the beginning and the end; not sustainable. You need to empower your team, something I work on every day.

On stress, if you know you're giving your best, and you're able to prioritize, then I don't get stressed if I'm leaving some things on the backburner. It's inevitable when the workload is heavy, and costs are tight.

Staying productive? They will always be highs and lows, but if you're in a job that you love, the highs are never far away."

CARLOS GARCIA PAVIA: "COVID has undoubtedly created new challenges to most of our schedules. We are likely to have to accommodate multiple zoom calls during the day that leave very little time to actually execute our core tasks. This causes increased stress and may push us to work after hours to catch up on the activities of the day.

We need to be more effective in managing our own schedules. You should feel empowered to block your calendar at different times of the day to accommodate the calls where you must be present and leave time to execute your core tasks of the day. Assign delegates to those calls where one of your directs will be well-positioned and appropriate to represent you. Avoid setting meetings for status reporting, and this can be done through a well-written and simplified periodic report, no need to meet for this.

Set clear agendas for every meeting, with clear objectives of the meeting and expected outcomes. Define actions with clear ownership and committed deadlines. Identify dependencies to execute on those actions and document them clearly, identifying accountable parties to drive communication with other participants that may not be present in the call. Do not assume that an action owner will read the minutes and react accordingly. Chase individually to ensure that the action owner is well-aware of what is expected."

Question 15: "What is your typical daily schedule? Do you have any hints for managing work-related stress? How do you stay productive?"

185

How can you apply these lessons and insights to your career or life today?

_____

_____

_____

_____

_____

_____

_____

_____

_____

_____

_____

_____

_____

It can be challenging to find time
for yourself in any career.
Do you have any
helpful tips on how to do this
successfully?

QUESTION 16

TADEO (JUN) CLARAVALL: "Self-care is not selfish. Finding time to take care of yourself and do things that revitalize you and make you happy is one of the highest return habits I've tried to practice in my life and work.

Think of it this way. When on airplanes, during the safety demonstrations before take-off, the flight steward tells you that in case of emergency, should the cabin lose pressure, oxygen masks will drop from the overhead area. The first thing we are told to do is assist our child, our elderly parent, or anyone else around us who needs help. Right? No, they don't.

They say, place the mask over your mouth and nose first BEFORE assisting others. Why? Because if you don't, then you'll pass out, and what good will you be to anyone at that point?

We can apply the same logic to daily life. We need to take care of ourselves first before we can take care of others.

One more thing, and I learned this the hard way.

Rest before you get tired. Don't wait until you need the rest. By that time, it's too late. You've already caused damage to yourself. You wouldn't drive your car without regular check-ups, would you? You wouldn't wait until your car breaks down; the gas tank goes on empty before you take care of it, would you? So why do we tend to wait until we feel burned out, sick, and tired before we take time to take care of ourselves?

My top tip: Block time daily for yourself and treat it with the same respect you would to an appointment with your boss or C.E.O. Use that time to do something that energizes you.

Also, do something fun. As the saying goes, "Life is Short, Eat Dessert First."

JESSICA HODSON: "This is a really hard thing, especially when you love what you do. My favorite tip is to be kind to yourself – if you know you spend all of Monday morning clearing emails, spend some time the

Question 16: "It can be challenging to find time for yourself in any career. Do you have any helpful tips on how to do this successfully?"

night before doing this so you can finish dead at 6 pm and have dinner with your family. Prioritize what is important to you and find a way to make this work."

JEROME MICHAILIDIS: "Yes. Have a realistic 'turn-off' time and place. Stick to them."

MARTIN JAMES WALLIS: "I have found it personally challenging to find the time. If I don't create the time at the start of the day, it is easy to overrun. I take time to meditate, read, learn, and take some form of physical exercise before starting my working day. It is not perfect, but this habit has helped me progress on some of the personal goals I have been working on. It may not be ideal for everyone. As we are still doing a lot of WFH, I have also begun to take a couple of breaks during the day to reset and re-align, making sure I can still be present. It is so easy to get into a task and realize that without any other personal interaction to break up your day, you haven't moved for two or three hours!"

ANTHONY NAPPI: "You have to make the time, think of this way, the company was there long before you came and will be there long after you leave, so plan a break. Come home early and take your significant other for dinner or lunch, your children to the park, go exercise, read a book or do whatever you find relaxing. Having some downtime is important for your health, your family and for yourself.

If all you do is work, eat, and sleep, over time, your productivity will slip, your attention to detail will falter, you will become angry and disillusioned. This will all impact your career and personal life – always keep in mind the values of family, health and faith – balance and perspective – we all have to work long and hard hours for periods of time, but if that is the norm, there is a bigger issue that should be addressed."

PAUL (PADDY) O'HARA: "Remember that the people that will remember you when you die will be your family and friends. They're more important than work will ever be. Easy to say and hard to do, but always keep it in the back of your mind."

JOHN CUSACK: "If you define happiness by how successful you are in your career, then this is not an issue. Suppose you don't (and I recommend you don't). In that case, reminding yourself regularly what makes you happy outside your career should be enough of an incentive to keep

Question 16: "It can be challenging to find time for yourself in any career. Do you have any helpful tips on how to do this successfully?"

189

those activities and hobbies alive. Covid 19 has given many of us the opportunity to prove we don't need to be seen all the time to be productive."

MEL GEORGIE B. RACELA: "I work a lot every weekday, from Monday to Friday. Saturday is treated as a transition from five (5) days of hard work to Sunday, which is definitely a family rest day, meaning whenever possible, I totally refrain from working or thinking about work; just peace, quietness, and rest with family. So, Saturday is quite flexible in that I do some work but at the same time do physical exercises and personal chores, like caring for my plants—a new hobby that I developed during the pandemic.

We are not machines, but then even machines are switched off periodically for maintenance. My tip, therefore, is: "After all the hard days' work, one must find time and indulge in a Sunday."

LUCY MASTERS: "During the working day, I block time for myself where I feel it is needed. I also carve out some restorative non-work time over the weekend, specifically including no screens. I find without any screens and lots of nature, my energy levels rise exponentially."

GUILLERMO HORTA: "All professionals need to take some time to recharge. Spend time with your loved ones and with your family. There is no position, no job and no income that will be valuable enough to replace those important moments with your family. Having clear agendas for meetings and establishing rules of the game with your team members is key, allowing everyone to recharge at the end of the day and during the weekends. Taking time off is imperative!"

SCOTT BURTON: "Communication is the key; by speaking to my team of staff, I am able to efficiently understand what challenges we have and what requires my time."

JAIKUMAR (JAI) RAMASWAMY: "Give the time you set aside for yourself or your family the same importance that you give to your most important meetings. For people who care about their work, it is often easy to justify shortchanging yourself or your family by missing an important personal event, taking time to think and reflect, or just taking some personal time to recharge to attend to critical work responsibilities. But it becomes increasingly difficult to keep yourself motivated without satisfying these parts of your life.

To avoid this, I make sure to block off time on my calendar for personal and family time — which includes time for personal thought and reflection — and treat that time as non-negotiable. There are always emergencies and urgent matters in the kind of work we do, so there is never a good time to care for yourself. But as a judge I once appeared before informed me: "no one is really indispensable" (this after I requested a continuance of a trial date for my wedding, and he told me to find another prosecutor to try the case). Of course, I don't mean that one should shirk their responsibilities — but learn to create boundaries."

CARLOS GARCIA PAVIA: "This is even more challenging when working from home. Have you wondered why productivity has been boosted during the past few months in 2020? Could it be because some of us are working without setting an out-of-office time? Quite possible.

We should make it a discipline to set a dedicated space to work, preferably a place that can be locked down after our out-of-office time. Giving the key to your spouse or partner to lock down your office may be a very good idea to prevent you from being tempted to go back to work. Some of us need to do this to change our self-inflicted workaholic habits."

Question 16: "It can be challenging to find time for yourself in any career. Do you have any helpful tips on how to do this successfully?"

191

REFLECTION

How can you apply these lessons and insights to your career or life today?

_____

_____

_____

_____

_____

_____

_____

_____

_____

_____

_____

_____

_____

If you could give advice to your younger self just entering our profession, what would it be?

QUESTION 17

TADEO (JUN) CLARAVALL: "I would say three things to the 20-year-old version of myself.

First, this too shall pass. Whatever you are going through, good or bad, it will pass. Stick to your principles no matter the cost.

Second, take more risks. Imagine what the realistic worst-case scenario is, determine to accept it and live with it if you must, then take the plunge. Don't overthink, and don't delay.

Third, engage with mentors, coaches, role models early and often. They may come in the form of people you meet, the books you read, learning programs you attend. Actively and frequently seek them out. Then take what you learn and try it out. If it fits, if it feels good, then keep doing it. If it doesn't, then discard it. But learn from other's successes and failures as often as possible. Learning by trial and error is a painful and inefficient way of learning. Yes, some lessons are best learned via personal discovery, but almost everything you are trying to do, someone else has done and has succeeded or failed at."

JEROME MICHAILIDIS: "Learn from everyone, no matter what their title or position."

MATT FRIEDMAN: "If I were able to provide advice to my younger self it would include the following ten statements: 1) find time to enjoy life; 2) be humble; 3) stay away from office politics and don't judge others; 4) never procrastinate – our lives unfold much faster than we expect; 5) spend time with people who are positive, supportive, encouraging, and compassionate; 6) never stop learning; 7) don't worry about what people think about you – walk your own path; 8) take time to get to know yourself; 9) always be willing to try and fail; and 10) put as much time into your personal life as you do with your professional life."

MEL GEORGIE B. RACELA: "I will tell myself to continue that path. There will be blood, sweat, and tears. But keep in mind that our profession is a public service, which makes it all the more worth enduring."

JOHN FOGARTY: "Understand data and technology and how humans interact with it. Build resilience quickly and don't take criticism personally."

JOHN CUSACK: "Try to experience as much of the pyramid as you can with spells in AML, Sanctions, Fraud, ABC, in Advisory & Controls, FIU, Risk Assessment, build a network, read and learn voraciously, work hard and be positive and have a can-do attitude. Add to this a real understanding of the business you are supporting, as well as complementary skills. These are the building blocks for a successful career. There are many reasons why your career won't be as successful as you'd like when you think it should be and others when it flies forward. Know there are no guarantees except failure if you don't try and have resilience."

PATRICIA SULLIVAN: "If you are committed to fighting financial crime and aspire to climb through the ranks to a leadership role, you need to think about how you can distinguish yourself. I see so many people who are so committed and entered the profession at junior ranks and it is really daunting and difficult to make your way up.

I benefitted by having the prosecutor credential, and others who join from a regulator have a similar edge. Still, suppose you don't have that. In that case, avenues to distinguish yourself could be a relocation opportunity where you might have a chance to be a bigger fish or put yourself out there in special initiatives that are important to your organization."

LUCY MASTERS: "Never forget your why! As financial crime fighters, we are fortunate to be very clear on that aspect. Always believe in yourself and follow your passion. Remain curious knowing that the work we do makes a difference in his world."

DR. WILLIAM SCOTT GROB: "There is a message of encouragement. Our industry is the custodian of the community. The news I would share with the anti-financial-crime community is that your actions matter.

I understand that many folks sit behind monitors doing work that seems unconnected with the crime happening outside. These individuals may be in a front-office support role collecting know-your-customer data or performing customer due diligence. It can appear a repetitive task where the data is collected, stored, and forgotten. For some financial institutions that have not connected their processes, this repetitive process may not be effective.

Don't be discouraged; work to improve the processes rather than criticize.

We lack a feedback loop that reinforces why we perform such extensive work connecting the dots around suspicious behavior. The work matters whether you sit in the front office, compliance, or audit.

We protect our companies, communities, and individuals. The rise of complicated crimes, such as modern slavery and human trafficking, requires a sophisticated response. An estimated 40 million people are trapped in modern slavery, through which organized crime earns annual profits of $150 billion. This crime is the third-largest source of dirty money.

What is alarming is that you can see modern slavery and human trafficking in every country in plain sight. The criminals are so brazen that they often operate openly, posting advertisements on the internet and social media—establishments operating at unusual hours and registering credit card payments in suspicious amounts, places, and operating times.

It can be easy to lose sight of what we're dealing with when talking about combating human trafficking. The criminal groups conduct this activity in an increasingly sophisticated and global manner. They can move people around the world to exploit in days, whereas investigations take time to complete.

This crime demonstrates the critical role compliance professionals play in combating the trade of human souls. We see the transactional data in near real-time. We must look at this issue as organized crime and terrorist groups invading our communities by abducting and exploiting the weak and vulnerable.

At the end of the process, our actions and the data collected fight these crimes and help protect our communities."

SCOTT BURTON: "Ongoing learning is critical to success and development. Try and understand trends and issues in the industry and be proactive in responding to these trends and issues is key. Identify role models and learn from their best behaviors and mistakes."

MAGGIE QIU: "I would tell my younger self to proactively find mentors and spend more time to maintain a sustainable relationship with them."

GUILLERMO HORTA: "Spend more time with your family and put aside the job responsibilities at certain times of the day. In my roles, I have

Question 17: "If you could give advice to your younger self just entering our profession, what would it be?"

always traveled half of my time, which unfortunately made me lose some important moments with my family and sacrificing important milestones in my daughter's school events. There is no job so important that you will need to sacrifice your family moments."

JESSICA HODSON: "The path upwards should always have a side-step. Remember to look around you at those better than you, and spend time watching and learning,

Sometimes going too fast can be a bad thing and leaves you underprepared for challenges you will face!"

JASON HOLT: "Treat everyone like they are a much-loved member of your family; when this is most difficult, you will reap the greatest rewards."

ANTHONY NAPPI: "Be patient and early in your career look to have as many different job experiences as possible to build a strong knowledge base, build your network and a better appreciation for what opportunities exist in the organization. Once you have found your passion focus on this area and build your career.

It is also important to understand that your career choices and what is important to you will not necessarily be the same things that are important to your colleagues, so do not benchmark against them, only against the person that looks at you in the mirror in the morning."

CARLOS GARCIA PAVIA: "I would imprint the message in my mind that debt is an enemy, savings are essential for life, and retiring at an early age makes total sense. I learned these principles from Dave Ramsey not long ago, and I wish I would have learned these principles a long time ago. These are now principles that I have passed on to my daughters, and I am sure that they will be working on building up their wealth to afford early retirement."

DEBORAH YOUNG: "Embrace change, read the room and help people adopt new ideas. Every challenge will have a learning, every learning will expand your mind, and with that knowledge, you can commit to impact and growth."

How can you apply these lessons and insights to your career or life today?

_____

_____

_____

_____

_____

_____

_____

_____

_____

_____

_____

_____

_____

If you had a chance to get a message out to all Financial Crime Fighters in the world, what would you write?

QUESTION 18

TADEO (JUN) CLARAVALL: "In life, at work, and in your relationships; Do what you resolve to do, NOW.

You said you wanted to learn more about financial crime technologies? Enroll in a course now.

Do you feel exhausted and want to take a break? Pause and take care of yourself now.

Do you want to go for that role that seems to be a stretch for you? Apply for it now.

Do you want to volunteer your time and expertise to charitable causes that you believe in? Reach out to those organizations now.

Do you want to confront a peer or colleague about their unacceptable behavior? Speak up now.

Do you want to tell someone how much their work, their help, their presence has helped you, or how much their friendship means to you? Tell them now.

No one is guaranteed a tomorrow. We only have today. We only have the present moment. How much longer are you going to wait?

Whatever it is you resolve to do, DO IT NOW.

I always keep a Stoicism coin near me. On the coin's face is engraved the message "Memento Mori", which is Latin for "remember you must die". It's my constant reminder that I can leave life right now. This reminder helps keep my life in perspective and helps guide my actions every day, so I do not procrastinate on what I already determined to be essential."

ANTHONY NAPPI: "Have the courage, discipline and conviction to always do what is right and never let anyone discourage you, pressure you not to do what you know is right or tell you what you are doing is not important. This can be difficult at times but is extremely important."

JOHN FOGARTY: "We are one, galvanized by a common purpose, only as strong as our weakest program. Strive for improvements, stay committed, and celebrate the successes when they come."

NICK TURNER: "Embrace technology. Let's have the computers do the tedious work for us, so we can focus on the interesting and fun stuff. I'd be happy for a computer to take over the boring parts of my job.

I also think more compliance people should take a crash course on databases. Once you understand how data is organized and moved around inside a bank, applying controls to it becomes much easier.

At the end of the day, financial crimes compliance is a lot about technology and finding suspicious patterns in our databases."

MATT FRIEDMAN: "Banks and other financial sector companies need to understand that by addressing the issue of modern slavery, they are not only protecting their business, they are also helping to address one of the biggest injustices of our time. The outcome will be that many people are freed from bondage. This makes their efforts TRULY HEROIC. Helping people to understand that they are heroic can be inspiring. It is a great way to help a community understand its true value. Following a banking event in Singapore, one of the participants said to me, "I felt really good after hearing you say how an ordinary banker can make a difference. I thought my job was meaningless. Now I realize it isn't. I am really grateful for this insight."

JASON HOLT: "Team up and kick proverbial!"

JESSICA HODSON: "It would be to remind that their skillset is an ever-evolving thing. The roles which we get through to recruit change or have different iterations almost every year.

Don't get complacent in your knowledge or development. Even the most senior of the people I speak to, are training and learning. Don't be afraid to look at something through a different lens – if this means asking others to help."

GUILLERMO HORTA: "Become true professionals. Keep learning about new industries and technologies. Keep an open mindset and fight for your dreams."

Question 18: "If you had a chance to get a message out to all Financial Crime Fighters in the world, what would you write?"

201

SCOTT BURTON: "You are lucky as you are doing what can be a relatively well-paid job, while at the same doing something that has a good public element to it and helping society by reducing the impact of financial crime."

MARLENE MELI: "The message would contain 3 points: First, to be passionate about what you do and always remember that behind each dollar laundered, there is a victim.

Secondly to continuously enhance your knowledge and skills to detect and stop financial crime. 3rd be proud of what you do and keep telling it."

PATRICIA SULLIVAN: "Working in FCC, particularly in a global bank, can be a wonderful opportunity to make a difference in creating better lives for victims of terrible crimes, prevent crimes from occurring, keep the banking sector safe and open for all, and along the way, have an exciting career in an environment with talented colleagues from all over the globe.

When I took that first FCC job in 2007, if you had told me that my FCC path would veer over the years to living in Hong Kong and London; traveling to so many wonderful parts of the globe; helping take down human trafficking and TF rings and advocating for tougher and more effective financial crime laws from Washington to Delhi to Vienna I surely would have thought you were crazy!"

MEL GEORGIE B. RACELA: "We are stronger together. The Philippines has always embraced collaboration, given the country's international commitments. The AMLC has been the co-chair of the Southeast Asia Counter-Terrorism Financing Working Group of the Financial Intelligence Consultative Group (FICG SEACTF WG) since 2018. Moreover, the Philippines, represented by the AMLC, is currently the sub-regional representative of the Asia/Pacific Group on Money Laundering (APG) Southeast Asia block."

JOHN CUSACK: "Read Teddy Roosevelt's "Man in the Arena" speech which of course must be read to include both men and women. I'd say be proud of what you do, not least recognize you are not a "timid soul" and that win or lose, for better or worse, you tried to make a difference despite the critics that have their say along the way. The speech included the following worthy of consideration, and I have found it so appropriate for the work of financial crime fighters. "It is not the critic who counts; not the man who points out how the strong man stumbles or where the doer of deeds could have done them better. The credit belongs to the man who is actually in the arena, whose face is marred by dust and sweat and blood; who strives valiantly; who errs, who comes short again and again, because there is no effort without error and shortcoming; but who does strive to do the deeds; who knows great enthusiasms, the great devotions; who spends himself in a worthy cause; who at best knows, in the end, the triumph of high achievement, and who at the worst, if he fails, at least fails while daring greatly, so that his place shall never be with those cold and timid souls who neither know victory nor defeat."

CARLOS GARCIA PAVIA: "Effectiveness is prime. Efficiency is important. Focus first on making your programs effective, then work on increasing efficiency without compromising effectiveness. Do not pursue efficiency targets at the expense of reducing the effectiveness of your programs or going beyond the boundaries of your risk appetite.

Include specific goals in the scorecards of your teams to assess alignment with risk appetite, process effectiveness, and proper governance. Achieving satisfactory ratings from internal and external reviewers is a collective responsibility; hold your teams accountable to do their part.

Most of all, enjoy what you do. Do it with full commitment and determination to do your best. What we all do is important; it matters now and for the future generations."

MARTA LIA REQUEIJO: "Mentorship, formal or informal, is essential."

PAUL (PADDY) O'HARA: "Try and make a difference to society, not just to the banks. Do it in your private life and do your own small bit to get the industry and governments around the world to start working together. No one will ever succeed on their own."

MAGGIE QIU: "Be confident that we are not a cost centre!"

LUCY MASTERS: "In flighting financial crime, I feel as though there are difficult decisions to be made every single day which require a great deal of considered thought and professional judgment. My personal approach to any such situation is to ensure I have considered many different perspectives and the impact of all potentially affected parties on any different decisions.

In order to do this, I enlist the help and input of others both within and outside of my direct team to ensure I am not driven by any unconscious bias I may not be aware of and have considered all angles. I don't make difficult decisions in a vacuum, and I am very comfortable being corrected or, indeed, wrong.

Also, a positive mindset in any situation, regardless of the obstacles faced, is key. Even though the fight against financial crime is a big one, and some challenges will take a concerted effort and time to address, I feel that having a positive approach is one less obstacle to deal with – oneself!

The other habit that has helped me is to approach any given situation with genuine curiosity. I have found this extremely valuable as in addition to learning and enriching my own understanding of a certain situation; people can intuitively sense when one is curious about learning more, as opposed to simply having an exchange to achieve a particular outcome, perhaps with an already pre-determined destination in mind!"

How can you apply these lessons and insights to your career or life today?

_____

_____

_____

_____

_____

_____

_____

_____

_____

_____

_____

_____

MENTOR INDEX

"Whatever it is you resolve to do,
DO IT NOW.

I always keep a Stoicism coin near me. On the coin's face is engraved the message "Memento Mori," which is Latin for "remember you must die." It's my constant reminder that I can leave life right now. This reminder helps keep my life in perspective and helps guide my actions every day, so I do not procrastinate on what I already determined
to be essential."

TADEO (JUN) CLARAVALL

FOUNDER, THE FINANCIAL CRIMES. FORMER MANAGING DIRECTOR, GLOBAL FINANCIAL CRIMES COMPLIANCE AT BANK OF AMERICA

TADEO (JUN) CLARAVALL

Jun is a student and teacher of financial crime risk and compliance and has invested over two decades of study and hands-on experience in the field of anti-financial crime.

He has spearheaded anti-money laundering, economic sanctions, anti-bribery and corruption programs for top-tier global financial institutions including Bank of America, JPMorgan Chase, UBS AG, and Citibank as a senior executive in the Asia Pacific region.

He has published technical articles on AML and has been invited numerous times as an expert resource speaker at international financial crimes conferences since 2007.

He is a Certified Public Accountant, Certified Internal Auditor, and Certified Anti-Money Laundering, Specialist.

In July 2019, Jun founded Global Financial Crimes Learning Technologies and had since dedicated his efforts to helping financial crime fighters gain higher-level skills, clarity, and confidence to fight financial crime through his consulting, workshops, and scorecard software.

He is also the host of The Financial Crimes Podcast, a podcast about financial crime fighters for financial crime fighters where he goes deep into the real skills needed to achieve success in our profession.

In addition to studying financial crimes, Jun is also an avid student of personal and professional growth. He loves to tease out from books and biographies the habits, routines, and lessons from world-class experts in business, leadership, and human potential.

"The why," is exactly what business management are desperate to understand, so they can help ensure that the controls they have in their businesses are actually dealing with the real risk, rather than being the result of a policy designed for one business line being applied inappropriately to another."

JASON HOLT

INTERIM GROUP HEAD OF GFCC AT A GLOBAL ASSET MANAGER

JASON HOLT

Jason is the interim Group Head of GFCC at a Global Asset Manager.

He was formerly the EMEA regional lead at Exiger, a global risk and compliance consulting firm that provides specialist financial crimes advisory, diligence, and technology solutions, to many of the world's largest and most complex financial institutions, corporations, governments, and supranational.

As a seasoned financial crimes risk management professional, Jason has spent the last 25 years at the forefront of the fight against financial crime. He has gained and shared a wealth of experience while working in a variety of roles, including at New Scotland Yard, where he was a dedicated financial investigator, working with the UK Courts to trace and recover the proceeds of crime from around the world.

Jason left law enforcement in 2001 and commenced a career in the private sector. Holding various senior financial crimes compliance roles, including as The Global Head of AML at Barclays, The EMEA Head of Financial Crimes Compliance at JP Morgan, and the International Head of Financial Crimes Compliance at Bank of America Merrill Lynch.

Jason has also had the privilege of playing a key role in a wide range of Industry initiatives and bodies, including The Wolfsberg Group, UK Joint Money Laundering Investigation Task Force (JMLIT), United for Wildlife, and more recently as a member of the Centre for European Policy Studies (CEPS) AML Task Force.

"In our field, one always has to have alternate solutions. Even if you are steadfast on backing 'choice A', you have to already consider choices B and C in case things don't work out."

JEROME MICHAILIDIS

HEAD OF NORMS AND PROCEDURES
AT BNP PARIBAS

JEROME MICHAILIDIS

Jerome is a seasoned professional in the Financial Security world and currently Head of Norms and Procedures at BNP Paribas. He has specialized in and led teams focusing on screening efficiency, policy creation, and effective training in his various positions.

His passion for his work and his management style incorporates his unique background, having studied Music and Linguistics before joining the Financial industry.

To Jerome, understanding people and their decisions are paramount. Considering multiple solutions is imperative. And understanding the complex world around us is both necessary and fun!

"I think becoming a specialist can sometimes close of avenues, rather than open them.
If you're really passionate about sanctions for example, do that and certainly specialise but try not to do so at a detriment to your more holistic financial crime knowledge.
Spend time working with your AML teams, or wider business to understand how sanctions is a cog in a wider financial crime risk assessment. People who can view a financial crime task with a wider lens, usually get the better result."

JESSICA HODSON

SENIOR HEADHUNTER PARTNER, INVESTIGO

JESSICA HODSON

Jessica has specialized in Financial Crime Compliance recruitment for the London market for over seven years. She is known for her candor, market knowledge, and technical understanding.

Jessica has some of the strongest networks in the sector because she has a real passion for enabling, enhancing, and advising her candidates on career moves for the long term.

The build of our financial crime functions is one of her specialties, and Jessica Hodson has been a part of and consulted on many firms on their financial crime structures. This has given her a unique perspective on what the sector looks for when hiring but also when strategizing financial crime functions.

"Of course there is more that can be done but there is also less. What's important is to find the right balance. We should be doing more of what makes sense and less of what doesn't. Before we can do this we need to define effectiveness and agree what the common purpose is. We can then promote and incentivise those actions that lead to measurable successes and retire or reduce those areas that don't."

JOHN CUSACK

CHAIR OF THE GLOBAL COALITION TO
FIGHT FINANCIAL CRIME

JOHN CUSACK

John has a wealth of experience in the Financial Crime world.

To start, he is Chair of the Global Coalition to Fight Financial Crime. John is also Editor and Founder of the Financial Crime News, Board Member of the anti-Human Trafficking -Traffic Analysis Hub, and Former Global Head Financial Crime Compliance at Standard Chartered Bank. In addition, he has been with the UBS for over 15 years and is a two-time Chair of the Wolfsburg Group.

Such experience finds John in several consultancy roles such as Adviser to Banks and Regtech Providers and promoting platforms and collaborations to improve effectiveness and modernize the fight against financial crime.

"'Data, Data, Data'. Clean, accurate and assured data from source systems cannot be underestimated. It is the foundation of all programs to fight financial crime. I have undertaken many remediation programs at large Banks and this is the one area that is so simple to say yet hard to achieve.
Process automation and capability can all be built around effective data management."

JOHN FOGARTY

EXECUTIVE GENERAL MANAGER FINANCIAL CRIME COMPLIANCE, AND MLRO AT THE COMMONWEALTH BANK OF AUSTRALIA

JOHN FOGARTY

John is currently the Executive General Manager of Financial Crime Compliance and MLRO at the Commonwealth Bank of Australia. John commenced his career in the NSW Police Force, finishing as a Detective Senior Constable in the Fraud Enforcement Agency.

Transitioning his knowledge in the criminal investigation into financial services Compliance and Anti Money Laundering, where over the past 26 years he has worked within Futures and Securities Exchanges, Investment Banks, Equities and Research companies, and Consumer Banks across Australia, South Asia, and Hong Kong.

"A positive mindset in any situation, regardless of the obstacles faced is key. Even though the fight against financial crime is a big one, and some challenges will take concerted effort and time to address, I feel that having a positive approach is one less obstacle to deal with - oneself!"

LUCY MASTERS

WESTPAC HEAD OF AUDIT COVERING FINANCIAL CRIME, COMPLIANCE AND CONDUCT AND SPECIALIST BUSINESSES

LUCY MASTERS

Lucy has over 25 years in the Financial Services Industry. Much of it is fighting financial crime via Internal Audit teams across professional firms and international banks based in Sydney, Singapore, London, and New Zealand.

Lucy is now Westpac Head of Audit covering Financial Crime, Compliance and Conduct and Specialist Businesses portfolios; before that, she was Head of Audit covering Consumer Bank, Finance, Operations, Business Bank and BT. Before Westpac, she worked in Citibank as the APAC and Japan Regional Head of Internal Audit for Compliance and AML, based initially in Singapore and then moving the role back to Australia in 2015.

Prior to Citi, Lucy worked at Barclays Bank PLC in both London and Singapore as an Internal Audit Director, responsible initially for Finance in London and then for Compliance and Central Functions for the APAC region. Before joining Barclays, she also worked for both Westpac Bank in Sydney Wellington, New Zealand, and before PwC in Sydney and London.

Outside of work, Lucy enjoys spending time with her husband, children, and Golden Retriever in Sydney's Northern Beaches. She is a volunteer surf lifesaver and ocean swimmer and loves their simple life in Australia after many years of living overseas.

"What was, and still is, most important for me to fight financial crime is the fact that behind every dollar laundered, there is a victim - a victim of drug trafficking and drug abuse, human trafficking, and slavery, of tax evasion and lack ofaccess to education."

MARLENE MELI

FINANCIAL CRIME MITIGATION
EXPERT

MARLENE MELI

Marlene is acknowledged for her track record to transfer regulatory requirements and FATF standards in AML, CFT, and KYC-CDD/EDD into operationally efficient and effective solutions at large national and international banks. In the last 30 years, she gained broad experience in Banking Operations, I.T., and Compliance at UBS and other international financial institutions.

For a couple of years, she works as an independent consultant in the area of financial crime mitigation. Based in Switzerland, she works closely with a global software firm providing anti-financial crime solutions. In this role, she consults the product team in developing and enhancing the solutions' capabilities to stay current with regulatory changes, the latest technology updates, and industry best practices. She also has mandates at Swiss banks in implementing anti-fraud solutions.

Before she became an entrepreneur, she was Head of Global Messaging & Screening Infrastructure at UBS with a special focus on sanctions screening and CFT.

Marlene is a Certified Anti-Money Laundering Specialist (CAMS) and holds a CAS International Compliance at Zurich University of Applied Sciences Management & Law and a B.A. at K.V. Zurich Business School.

Furthermore, Marlene is a founding board member of the ACAMS (Association of Certified Anti-Money Laundering Specialists) Switzerland Chapter and speaker at ACAMS events in Asia.

"By keeping the social impact of financial crime in mind and trying to make a difference where you can, however small, means you are creating a positive to counter these negatives. This is one of the core elements I have observed across the industry, the desire to do better. This is a very unifying ideal and manifests in the discussions around best practices and knowledge sharing and keeps the momentum moving forward."

MARTIN JAMES WALLIS

CHIEF OPERATING OFFICER,
FINTRAIL

MARTIN JAMES WALLIS

Martin is a naturally curious problem solver who relishes the professional challenges that the fight against global financial crime creates. Drawing on a wealth of experience from the public sector, Martin combines this with growing industry knowledge to provide intelligent, inclusive, and business-focused solutions to the FinTech sector in support of the fight against global financial crime.

Based in Singapore, Martin has a real passion for Southeast Asia and the vibrant FinTech ecosystem that is developing within the region. As the Head of Operations, he is also focused on scaling FINTRAIL across Europe, the US, APAC, the Middle East, and Africa.

Before joining FINTRAIL, Martin had an extensive career within the British Army Intelligence Corps, serving as an analyst, operator, instructor, and manager in specialist intelligence and security roles supporting military operations worldwide.

"After significant trial and error over the years across people, process, and technology I have a strong view that the private sector will only succeed in identifying and stopping meaningful financial crime issues by working in legal frameworks that support proactive intelligence sharing B2B and public sector to private."

PATRICIA SULLIVAN

GLOBAL HEAD OF FINANCIAL CRIME
BUSINESS CONTROL & OVERSIGHT,
DEUTSCHE BANK

Patricia Sullivan

Patricia has more than 20 years of experience in Financial Crime Compliance (FCC) on both the private and public sides across the globe, having lived and worked in the US, Hong Kong, and the UK. From 2014 to February 2021, Ms. Sullivan was at Standard Chartered Bank, leading the Global FCC program.

Before joining Standard Chartered, Ms. Sullivan was Deputy Global Head of FCC and APAC Head of FCC for UBS based in Hong Kong. In March 2021, Ms. Sullivan launched the FCC Partnership Group, LLC to provide best-in-class FCC services to governments and private entities.

Ms. Sullivan also serves on the Executive Board of Lawyers Without Borders, a non-profit devoted to advancing the rule of law initiatives across the globe.

"Governance and Oversight are critical. Equally, it highlights the importance of having the correct risk decisioning framework in place with the correct people making reasonable risk decisions that are well documented. This protects the firm but also protects you as an individual."

ROD FRANCIS

SENIOR MANAGING DIRECTOR AND ASIA LEAD FOR THE FINANCIAL CRIME COMPLIANCE PRACTICE AT FTI CONSULTING

ROD FRANCIS

Rod is a Senior Managing Director and Asia lead for the Financial Crime Compliance practice at FTI Consulting and is based in Hong Kong.

Rod is a senior compliance professional with a career in the financial services industry spanning 30 years.

Twenty-five of those years have been spent in risk management-related roles covering various business sectors and products, including Consumer/Retail, Wholesale, Corporate and Investment, Wealth Management, and Asset Management Banking.

For the last 11 years, Rod has been based in Hong Kong, covering the Asia Pacific region, and before this, he was based in London, covering Europe, Middle East, and Africa (EMEA).

Before joining FTI Consulting, Rod was Citibank's APAC Anti-Money Laundering (AML) Compliance Head for eight years. This role also encompassed responsibility for AML Compliance for the Global Consumer Bank for EMEA. In this role, Rod was the senior executive leader responsible for and instrumental in leading Citibank's successful AML change program in response to US regulatory commitments. During this period, Rod also had responsibility for Economic Sanctions Compliance and Anti-Bribery & Corruption.

In the Asia Pacific, Rod also worked for UBS, where he held several senior management positions, including APAC Head of Central Compliance. He was responsible for establishing and implementing the unit in APAC and as a global unit for Regulatory Reporting. During his time at UBS, Rod was also UBS's APAC Head of Anti-Money Laundering and Sanctions Compliance.

Before 2007, Rod was based in London, covering the EMEA region working for tier one banks. Amongst compliance roles for financial institutions, Rod was the EMEA Regional Head of AML and Sanctions for both Credit Suisse and Morgan Stanley, incorporating Central Compliance and Operations Compliance for each, respectively. Rod implemented Morgan Stanley's first EMEA regional AML Compliance function and assisted Credit Suisse in EMEA re-designing its regional AML program focusing on both efficiency and effectiveness.

Rod has a broad in-depth knowledge and experience in anti-money laundering, sanctions, and anti-bribery compliance is a member of the Association of Certified Anti-Money Laundering Specialists (ACAMS) and the Director of Membership Board Member of the Hong Kong Chapter of ACAMS. Rod regularly speaks at industry events, including ACAMS seminars.

"Ongoing learning is critical to success and development. Try and understand trends and issues in the industry and be proactive in responding to these trends and issues is key. Identify role models and learn from their best behaviors and mistakes."

SCOTT BURTON

ASIA PACIFIC HEAD OF ANTI-FINANCIAL CRIME DEUTSCHE BANK

SCOTT BURTON

Scott started his career at Anderson consulting. He joined Credit Suisse in 1998, where he worked in various roles, including the regional head of AML.

After 15 years in Credit Suisse, Scott joined JP Morgan as regional head of FCC, where he built out a significant size team of over 130 people over a seven-year period. In 2017 Scott joined Deutsche Bank as Regional Head of Anti-Financial Crime, APAC.

"The anti-financial crime responsibilities must be across the entire financial institution at all levels. Everyone commits to fight financial crime. Unfortunately, some people do not recognize the duty. They may focus on profit above all else. Their view espouses maximizing profits and shareholder value. While many companies have this goal in their metric, it is an incomplete goal because it ignores the more significant issues of financial crime."

DR. WILLIAM SCOTT GROB

ACAMS AML DIRECTOR FOR
THE AMERICAS

DR. WILLIAM SCOTT GROB

William, CAMS-FCI, CGSS, FRM, CAIA, is the ACAMS AML Director for the Americas, having been the AML Director in APAC for the last three years, responsible for developing regional anti-financial crime content strategy and implementing new content.

In his role, he has built customized programs, such as the Stop Illegal Wildlife Trade certificate being developed jointly with the WWF and Ending Modern Slavery & Human Trafficking with the FAST Initiative.

William has over 25 years of financial and banking expertise working in various compliance and risk management roles at HSBC and Deutsche Bank. He presents at regional conferences, symposiums, and webinars on various topics, such as the Sunrise Series for VASPs, policy and regulatory issues, and training gaps in the industry.

"In order to stay relevant, and effective, in detecting and preventing financial crime to address the advances in technology and typologies, we need to recognize no one segment can transform on its own and we will have to think beyond the existing methods."

STEVENSON MUNRO

GLOBAL HEAD, ECONOMIC SANCTIONS COMPLIANCE, HIGH RISK CLIENTS AND EMERGING THREATS - GROUP FINANCIAL CRIME COMPLIANCE TEAM

STEVENSON MUNRO

Steven joined Standard Chartered Bank in July 2015 as the Global Head of Sanctions Compliance, after having held senior financial crime compliance leadership positions within three other global financial institutions focusing on the strategy, program design, and implementation of anti-corruption, economic sanctions, and anti-money laundering compliance programs. He works closely with industry peers to inform the broader community of compliance professionals and policymakers about the strategies for effective financial crime and sanctions compliance in a global context and the nuances and complexities of implementing international sanctions compliance programs coordinated across multiple lines of business.

Prior to entering the private sector, Mr. Munro served as Deputy Chief Counsel for U.S. Treasury's Office of Foreign Assets Control (OFAC), providing legal counsel to OFAC and the U.S. Treasury Department related to the development, implementation, and enforcement of foreign policy based economic sanctions programs. For more than 20 years, STEVENSON MUNRO has focused on combatting financial crime and enhancing the profession of financial crime compliance.

He earned his law degree from New York University School of Law, has a Master of Science in strategic intelligence from the Defence Intelligence College, and a Bachelor of Science in economics from the Wharton School at the University of Pennsylvania. He is certified by the Association of Certified Anti-Money Laundering Specialists (ACAMS).

Mr. Munro started his career as a military intelligence officer in the U.S. Army, holding positions focused on contingency planning for both tactical and strategic operations, including a posting to the White House Military Office's Presidential Emergency Operations Centre.

"An organization's talent strategy is a key weapon in its financial crime-fighting armoury. As a recruitment professional, I believe it's the most important aspect to achieving more within Financial Crime Compliance departments. While this will be dependent on the budget, a pro-active hiring plan should be a part of any overall organizational development strategy."

WILL BROWN

HEAD OF CORPORATE GOVERNANCE
RECRUITMENT HAMLYN WILLIAMS

WILL BROWN

Will is currently overseeing the Financial Services executive search practice for Hamlyn Williams across the U.S., with a core focus on Compliance and Financial Crime Compliance.

Will has previously led the Compliance and FCC practices in the U.S, APAC, and EMEA for Hamlyn Williams. This is a full-service recruitment firm specializing across all regulated industries globally and with a core focus on Financial Services, Technology, and Pharmaceutical spaces.

"Awareness and communication are also key; you need the business's buy-in, and to achieve that, you need to successfully 'sell' the idea of compliance. This means being able to work collaboratively with the business and present 'the financial crime world' in a narrative consumable by non-financial crime experts."

MARTA LIA REQUEIJO

HEAD OF FINANCIAL CRIME COMPLIANCE AND MONEY LAUNDERING REPORTING OFFICER FOR CLEARBANK UK.

MARTA LIA REQUEIJO

Marta is an accomplished senior financial crime and compliance director with over 17 years of leadership experience in the financial services industry.

Marta is currently the Head of Financial Crime Compliance and Money Laundering Reporting Officer for ClearBank UK. She has spent her professional career shaping compliance and anti-financial crime frameworks in global organizations and Fintech companies.

Marta has vast experience leading the design or enhancement of financial crime compliance frameworks. She advises businesses and executive teams on their business growth strategy, enabling scalable and automated controls for long-term operational effectiveness and efficiency by helping to create solutions that positively impact customer experience.

She has held senior leadership positions in the banking and payment sectors in the U.K. and Portugal at Citigroup, HSBC, Worldpay, GoCardless, Novo Banco Bank, and Caixa Geral de Depositos Bank. She also operated in a regulatory capacity at the Portuguese Securities Market Commission to regulate and supervise Financial Institutions in relation to Money Laundering and Compliance.

Marta is a tutor for the International Compliance Association's Professional Postgraduate Diploma in Financial Crime Compliance. As a passionate mentor, Marta helps the next generation of talented young individuals to realize their potential. She is an Advisory Board member of the U.K. registered charity "Migrant Leaders," which mentors first and second generations of young migrants living in the U.K. While not working, you can spot her enthusiasm for new adventures as she travels the world with her cherished camera in hand and with her daughter, Madalena, as her "partner in crime."

"All too often, when things go wrong it's the shareholders that bare the impact with falling share prices, cancelled dividends, costly fines and remediation / transformation programs going on for years and years, so I would like to see the increase in personal civil and criminal liability on Directors and employees, in the cases of wilful blindness, negligence, incompetence or all three."

ANTHONY QUINN

FOUNDER AT ARCTIC INTELLIGENCE

ANTHONY QUINN

Anthony has over 20 years of consulting experience, starting his career in London working in the capital markets practice of Accenture for 7 years.

During this time Anthony was responsible for leading a number of high-profile transformation programs for clients including Goldman Sachs, Morgan Stanley, JP Morgan, ING, Schroders Investment Management, and the Bank of New York.

In 2003, Anthony moved to Australia and was involved in leading several risks and compliance transformation programs at the National Australia Bank and Westpac.

In 2006, Anthony was headhunted by Macquarie Bank as the Program Director, responsible for delivering the anti-money laundering and counter-terrorism financing program for the banking and financial services division. Anthony also ran the FATCA (tax evasion compliance) program for the same division for 3 years.

In 2015, whilst working at Macquarie Bank, Anthony founded Arctic Intelligence (www.arctic-intelligence.com), a RegTech business focused on audit, risk, and compliance software related to financial crime risk management.

In 2016, Anthony co-founded AML Accelerate as part of a joint venture which was acquired by Arctic Intelligence in 2018.

In 2020, Arctic Intelligence was awarded the Australian Founded RegTech of the Year and Exporter of the Year by the Australian RegTech Association.

"Banks and other financial sector companies need to understand that by addressing the issue of modern slavery, they are not only protecting their business, they are also helping to address one of the biggest injustices of our time. The outcome will be that many people are freed from bondage. This makes their efforts TRULY HEROIC."

MATT FRIEDMAN

CEO, THE MEKONG CLUB AND MODERN SLAVERY EXPERT

Matt Friedman

Matt is a leading, internationally renowned global expert on modern slavery and human trafficking. An award-winning public speaker, author, filmmaker, and philanthropist, Matt regularly advises heads of governments, banks, and intelligence agencies. As the founder and CEO of The Mekong Club, Matt is considered the leading catalyst of the anti-slavery movement in Asia's business sector by captains of industry.

He has managed and directed tens of millions of dollars to major humanitarian portfolios impacting millions of people for the U.S. State Department (USAID) and the United Nations. His work over the last 35 years of pioneering and managing international anti-human trafficking and public health programs in over 40 countries has given him access to many influential networks in different countries throughout the world.

Matt is the author of 13 books ranging from action novels, non-fiction accounts of his human rights work, to a book that outlines his unique philosophy of "time."

Matt won the prestigious 2017 Gold Standard Award for Asia Communicator of the Year — "Because of Matthew's absolute commitment to the issue and his tireless drive to reach as many people as he can, he is Communicator of the Year." Matt was an executive producer and advisor on four award-winning films, one of which was nominated for an Emmy.

Each year, Matt has cited an average of 40 times in the news media (e.g. CNN, Bloomberg, Reuters, Associated Press, the Financial Times, the Economist, and more).

"It is never easy and what is most difficult is to convince others that there may be an anti-money laundering issue in a transaction or in parties one is dealing with.
What is important is to ensure you have clearly studied any transaction or issues carefully and carried out due diligence and then convince others with the facts."

YVETTE CHEAK

SEASONED BANKING COMPLIANCE
PROFESSIONAL IN SINGAPORE

Yvette Miriam Yat Ying,

Yvette has over 40 years of experience in the financial industry ranging from Retail & Consumer Banking, Capital Market, Finance Companies, and Trade Finance both in the Public and Private Sectors.

In recent years she has been actively involved in the evolution of AML/CFT Standards of Compliance in Singapore and the Region.

Yvette chaired the Association of Bank in Singapore (ABS) Self-Governance and Compliance Standing Committee for many years until her retirement and is currently still serving as Adviser to the ABS.

"A healthy and robust FC program has a research and development component constantly scanning the environment for emerging threats and regular diagnostics assessing any vulnerabilities arising from changes to the business model, evolving client needs and the need to maintain competitiveness. Without this, a colleague of mine often refers to this as a battle between organized crime and disorganized banks."

ERIC FAVILA

SENIOR PRINCIPAL PROMONTORY
FINANCIAL GROUP

ERIC FAVILA

Eric is a Senior Principal in Promontory's Singapore office focused on risk management and preventing financial crime. He advises financial institutions and regulators in the Asia Pacific on enhancing their risk governance framework, specializing in the prevention of financial crime. He has lead engagements in the region, ranging from remediation projects to the design of full-scale AML/CFT programs.

Eric has also dedicated time to advising policymakers, law enforcement, journalists, and NGO's in the financial processes to limit the prevalence of the Online Sexual Exploitation of Children (OSEC). He is a member of the External Advisory Council of the International Justice Mission (IJM) Scale of Harm Project with the aim to develop methods to estimate the prevalence of trafficking.

Prior to joining Promontory, Eric was a Director for Risk Solutions at Standard&Poor's where he was responsible for the credit risk modeling advisory practice. He was also responsible for delivering rating solutions and financial data platforms across Southeast Asia.

Eric holds a Bachelor's degree in Management Engineering from Ateneo de Manila University and an MBA from INSEAD.

"A well-informed Board and executive is a must as well as the people who can impact widespread change. The decision to equip line managers with the right RegTech tools to manage the risks must be made whether this uses AI, machine learning, NLP or blockchain."

DEBORAH YOUNG

FOUNDING CEO OF THE REGTECH ASSOCIATION

DEBORAH YOUNG

Deborah is the founding CEO of The RegTech Association, a global non-profit industry member body focussed on accelerating the adoption of RegTech solutions and creating an international center of excellence. Since helping to establish the Association in 2017, she has led the growth of 180 organizations, including 130 RegTech firms.

Deborah has led the recognition of Australia as the third-highest concentration of RegTech producers in the world. The cohort also includes top-tier banks, global technology companies, and consulting firms. She has advocated for the industry with the Government, regulators, investors, and trade agencies.

Deborah sits on the Australian Federal Government FinTech Advisory Committee, NSW Government ICT Procurement Task Force, The National Blockchain Roadmap RegTech Committee and, is a member of the ASIC Digital Committee. In addition, she is a regular global speaker, presenter, and designer of RegTech programs for the Association and its partners and with regulators in Australia and overseas.

Deborah is an accomplished chief executive, non-executive director, mentor, and strategic business consultant. She has over 20 years of experience as a senior executive across financial services, including investment banking, private equity, venture capital, superannuation, and insurance spectrums. Deborah holds an Executive MBA (Global) from UTS Business School and was named as the Australian Financial Review's 100 Women of Influence in 2019 for Innovation.

"Perhaps the most difficult part of fighting financial crime is to balance the effectiveness of the compliance programs and the ability to operate with minimum customer friction. This becomes even more important in the world that is becoming more and more digitalized every day."

CARLOS GARCIA PAVIA

GLOBAL HEAD OF SCREENING, SURVEILLANCE, AND
REGULATORY CONDUCT ANALYTICS

CARLOS GARCIA PAVIA

Carlos is a Senior Financial Crime Compliance Executive helping global organizations to build, run and innovate Financial Crime Risk, Sanctions Compliance, and Risk Analytics programs that effectively address regulatory requirements while increasing operational efficiency and maintaining an appropriate risk appetite with sound governance and controls. His area of focus is Screening Technology and Analytics in Financial Services.

From the start of his career 30 years ago with the largest I.T. Consulting firm in Mexico City, Carlos has progressively transitioned through multiple roles in I.T., Operations, FCC, and Risk Analytics, having the opportunity to contribute with some of the largest financial institutions and digital companies in Mexico, the USA, and the U.K. Carlos has had multiple contributions to major publications and media channels, delivering insight on Financial Crime Compliance in the Americas.

He currently serves as Global Head of Screening, Surveillance, and Regulatory Conduct Analytics at one of the largest global banks in the U.K., where he leads a team of data scientists and other analytics professionals specialized in the optimization of analytics products and models supporting Compliance programs using diverse Artificial Intelligence and Machine Learning technologies.

Carlos holds an Electronics Engineering degree from Universidad Autonoma Metropolitana in Mexico City. Carlos enjoys sharing his professional and life experiences with young professionals worldwide through mentoring and coaching to help them reach their full potential.

"Work in a company where your values are aligned. If you wake up in the morning and don't want to go to work, it's time to find something else."

PAUL (PADDY) O'HARA

FORMER HEAD OF FCC FOR STANDARD CHARTERED BANK

PAUL (PADDY) O'HARA

Formerly Head of FCC for Standard Chartered Bank, PAUL (PADDY) O'HARA was based in Hong Kong, where he has been for 17 years.

From 1997 – 2013, he worked for JP Morgan in Hong Kong, London, and Singapore, with roles relating to financial crime, client due diligence, and fraud investigation.

Prior to this, he spent six years in the Royal Hong Kong Police, specializing in Fraud Investigation.

His first job was as a Constable in the Metropolitan Police in London, first as a bobby on the street, and latterly with the local drug squad.

He has two daughters, growing up too fast, and a very patient wife.

"I think of it as very similar to seat belt use and car crash prevention. It makes no sense to wait until you have been in a car crash to start using a seat belt, which can prevent or reduce injury in the unlikely event your car is in an accident. It is for this reason that it doesn't make sense to wait until you have, or your employer has, been affected directly by financial crimes to take steps to prevent or detect such activity."

ARMINA ANTONIOU

GM FINANCIAL CRIME RISK AT TABCORP (AUSTRALIA)

ARMINA ANTONIOU

Armina has more than 20 years of experience as a Risk and Legal professional with a broad cross-section of Australian and Global companies.

Currently, Armina is the General Manager of Financial Crime Risk at Tabcorp, leading a Financial Crime specialist team. Tabcorp is Australia's biggest listed gambling and entertainment company and one of the biggest gambling companies in the world.

Armina leads the engagement with law enforcement and Australia's FIU and AML/CTF regulator – AUSTRAC – including within AUSTRAC's public-private partnership, the Fintel Alliance, and oversees Tabcorp's AML/CTF and Sanctions compliance programs.

Armina has led and sponsored the financial crime work programs across multiple integration programs at Tabcorp to ensure standardized training, operational, and systems-based compliance procedures across more than 4,400 retail bet selling outlets and one of Australia's largest online betting operators.

Armina is Tabcorp's Inclusion Ambassadors, a proud soccer mum, and a huge sports fan.

"Criminal organizations move on a super-fast speed. By the time banks identify a typology and establish reasonable controls to mitigate such risks, organized crime is already finding new ways to move the money, to overtake controls and to identify the banks that have a weaker AML Program which will facilitate the disguise of illicit funds."

GUILLERMO HORTA

GLOBAL HEAD AND CHIEF ANTI-MONEY
LAUNDERING OFFICER - SCOTIABANK
INTERNATIONAL BANK

GUILLERMO HORTA

Before joining ScotiaBank, Guillermo was the Head of Financial Crimes Compliance for UBS AG Americas. Previously, Guillermo held several positions with Bank of America Merrill Lynch, including Managing Director and Global Senior Executive of Financial Crimes Compliance and Head of Financial Crimes Compliance for the Americas.

Guillermo also held several positions within the Legal and Compliance Units at Citigroup, including Managing Director and Head of Anti-Money Laundering and Economic Sanctions for Mexico and Latin America.

Guillermo is constantly invited as a keynote speaker to AML related international forums. He is an active member of several AML and Banking associations where he has occupied the positions of President of the Anti-Money Laundering Committee of the Latin American Banks Federation (FELABAN); Chairman of the Compliance Committee of the Mexican Banks Association (ABM); the current Co-Chair of the Anti-Money Laundering Committee of the Florida Bankers Associations (FIBA) and former President of the Latin America Task Force of ACAMS.

Guillermo has a J.D degree in Law from the Universidad Iberoamericana Tijuana, and has postgraduate studies in Criminal Law and Telecommunications Law.

Before his financial sector career, Guillermo worked in a government agency involved in topics related to justice procurement and as an Associate in a prestigious international law firm in Mexico City.

"You can have the best year financially, but one significant control break, whether that be AML, fraud or another event negates all the positive work that was done."

ANTHONY J. NAPPI

FORMER CITIBANK GLOBAL HEAD OF
OPERATIONAL RISK AND CONTROL FOR
THE CONSUMER BANK

ANTHONY J. NAPPI

Anthony is an experienced Senior Executive with extensive experience across a wide range of businesses and functions, including international assignments in Singapore and Hong Kong. His background includes Corporate and Consumer Banking, leading large complex businesses, Operations, Technology, Human Resources, Operational Risk Management, Compliance, Strategic Planning, Financial Control, Customer Service and Sales.

He is currently acting as an advisor to two start-up companies - Transcontinental University and MommyDaddy&Me, an online educational company. He is also mentoring a number of individuals, which is a passion he has to help people grow in their careers.

"One common mistake I saw is that financial crime fighters often walk the walk, but not talk the talk. What I mean by that is that they often are hardworking people but often not paying attention to the importance of communication.
Whether it is to explain to regulators and auditors or educate and discuss with internal stakeholders, they are not always good at telling the stories and articulate the risks in a direct, in an easy-to-understand manner."

MAGGIE QIU

HEAD OF SANCTIONS OF GREATER CHINA AND NORTH ASIA AT STANDARD CHARTERED BANK

MAGGIE QIU

Maggie is the Head of Sanctions of Greater China and North Asia at Standard Chartered Bank. She has the responsibilities of managing the Sanctions and BIS Compliance Program for the region.

Prior to joining Standard Chartered, she was the Regional Program Director, Global Financial Crimes Compliance for Bank of America Merrill Lynch. She was responsible for regulatory exams, audit, regulatory changes, compliance Monitoring & Testing, issue management, Policy and Program, Risk Assessments, and the training of 12 jurisdictions in the Asia Pacific region.

Before relocating to Hong Kong in January 2014, Ms Qiu was the Head of FCC & MLRO for Bank of American China and led BAML's Anti-Money Laundering and Economic Sanctions efforts for all of the branches in China. She was in that role since 2010, and previously, Ms Qiu worked for the Financial Intelligence Unit (FIU) in Bank of American's Global Headquarter in Charlotte, NC.

Before joining Bank of America Merrill Lynch, Ms Qiu also held various risk management roles in Wachovia and Wells Fargo in the United States. She received a Master's degree from the University of Illinois Urbana-Champaign, USA.

Maggie is a frequent speaker at international seminars and conferences for Financial Crimes Compliance, Sanctions, regulatory compliance for Fintech and digital assets, also an early investor in Bitcoin.

"We continue to educate and learn, collaborate, and partner as well as commit until we see the fruits of our labor, which is depriving the criminals of the profits of their crime.

By repetitively doing ECC, we strike criminals where it hurts the most: their proceeds of crime, their sources of funding, illegal assets, and financial transactions.

Ultimately, this not only maintains the integrity of domestic and international financial systems, but also decreases lawlessness, thus protecting the common good."

MEL GEORGIE B. RACELA

EXECUTIVE DIRECTOR, AMLC
SECRETARIAT

MEL GEORGIE B. RACELA

As head of the Anti-Money Laundering Council's (AMLC) operational arm, Executive Director Mel has been executing the AMLC's vision and ensuring sustainable reforms for the Secretariat since 2017. Before this, he held positions in the Bangko Sentral ng Pilipinas for 21 years in the areas of banking supervision, legal counseling, litigation, and financial investigation.

Mel contributed largely to legislative and regulatory framework developments, filling critical gaps in the Philippines' anti-money laundering and counter-terrorism financing (AML/CTF) defense. This included the Republic Act No. (RA) 10927, known in local parlance as the Casino Law; RA 11479 or the Anti-Terrorism Act of 2020; RA 11521, which recently amended the Anti-Money Laundering Act of 2001; and their respective Implementing Rules and Regulations.

Further, under Mel's supervision was the approval of the Second National Risk Assessment Report, which evaluated the overall threat and effectiveness of the Philippines' AML/CTF mechanisms; and the approval of Executive Order No. 68 series of 2018 by the President, which embodies the country's National AML/CTF Strategy (NACS). The NACS adopts a whole government approach to coordinate efforts of the government and the private sector in combating money laundering and terrorism financing in the country.

A lawyer and a certified public accountant, Mel also holds a Master of Laws degree in International Legal Studies from Georgetown University Law Center in Washington, DC, USA, where he graduated a Dean's Lister. He obtained his Bachelor of Laws degree from San Beda College and his Accounting degree from De La Salle University in the Philippines.

"Financial institutions play an enormously important gatekeeping role in preventing and detecting illicit financial activity and compliance failure can compromise the effectiveness of the system that we have created globally to combat it.
However, during my time at DOJ it become increasingly clear that enforcement can only be part of the solution - it is as important for financial institutions to create the right culture to support a financial crimes compliance program."

JAI RAMASWAMY

CHIEF RISK & COMPLIANCE
OFFICER AT cLABS

Jaikumar (Jai) Ramaswamy

Jai is the Chief Risk & Compliance Officer at cLabs, a startup developing software applications on Celo, an open-source, distributed ledger protocol designed to create a more accessible financial system. Before joining cLabs, he was the Head of Enterprise Risk Management at Capital One and the Global Head of AML Compliance Risk Management at Bank of America/Merrill Lynch.

Before joining the private sector, Jai served as the Chief of the Asset Forfeiture and Money Laundering Section at the Department of Justice and prosecuted complex fraud and cybercrime cases as an Assistant United States Attorney for the Southern District of New York and a trial attorney with the DOJ's Computer Crime and Intellectual Property Section.

While at the Department of Justice, Jai oversaw the prosecutions of BNP Paribas, HSBC, Standard Chartered, ING, and the virtual currency provider Liberty Reserve for AML and Sanctions violations. Jai has an undergraduate degree from Harvard University, a law degree from the University of Pennsylvania Law School, and a doctorate in political science from Cambridge University, UK.

"I have witnessed the agility and resources criminals have at their disposal. Therefore, providing an adequate level of counter crime fighting also requires the same level of nimbleness and tenacity. Sharing of information, best practices, risk, compliance, and auditing approaches, and identifying emerging risks across industry and amongst our peers is a key critical component to aiding a globally accepted strategy to fight financial crime."

ABTAR RANDHAWA

GLOBAL FINANCIAL CRIME AUDIT
EXECUTIVE

Abtar Randhawa

Abtar is a versatile and articulate executive-level audit, risk, and compliance professional, who gained his skills working at the world's leading corporates.

Abtar led specialist teams across three defense lines undertaking complex work programs in multiple sectors in the leading financial services hubs (London, NY, Singapore, and Sydney).

Abtar possesses board and senior-level engagement skills, delivering key messages and strategies to assist executives in enterprise-wide change.

"Personal achievement is personal. If it means being visible or leading a team, that's great. If it means leaving time for family, friends, and hobbies, that's also great.
My suggestion would be to think about what fulfillment is, commit to it, and accept that it might change over time. Whatever success is, it can't be measured in overtime or dollars."

NICK TURNER

OF COUNSEL IN THE HONG KONG
OFFICE OF STEPTOE & JOHNSON

NICK TURNER

Nick Turner is a New York-qualified lawyer living and working in Hong Kong, specializing in economic sanctions and anti-money laundering compliance and investigations. Nick began his financial crime-fighting career with Citi in New York and California.

He then moved to Hong Kong to work as a regional sanctions compliance officer. Eventually, he found his way into a law firm where he began advising clients on complying with U.S. laws and regulations.

He is currently Of Counsel in the Hong Kong office of Steptoe & Johnson, a Washington, DC-based law firm. In addition to advising clients on the meaning of laws and regulations, Nick helps clients conduct internal investigations of compliance breaches and communicates on their behalf with the U.S. government and other authorities.

In his early career, Nick worked as a newspaper journalist, a public relations intern, an advertising copywriter, and as a project coordinator for a non-profit foundation, as well as a freelance writer. Later on, he decided to attend law school, where he developed his interest in international law and regulation, leading him to where he is today.

Nick grew up in Nebraska, in the United States, and has lived in New York, Washington, DC, Los Angeles, and Hong Kong. For fun, Nick writes a weekly briefing called the "Sanctions Top-5," where he shares his thoughts on the latest developments in economic sanctions.

He is looking forward to reconnecting with his colleagues and friends in the community of financial crime throughout Asia once international travel returns to normal.

YOUR TURN

It is your turn to answer the 18 questions.

You have read the responses from the 30 senior leaders. Now it is time to write your responses to the same 18 questions. Use the spaces provided to write down your answers. Then utilise your responses as daily inspiration and guidance for the financial crime fighter you are and are continually becoming.

You may email your responses to me at book@thefinancialcrimes. com. I will read all of them. If there is a volume 2 of this book, I might ask you to be in it, or I might invite you to guest in The Financial Crimes podcast so you can share the story of how you acted on the lessons from this book and how that changed your life and career.

How did you start your Financial Crime Fighting career?
What inspired you to take this course in life?

_____

_____

_____

_____

_____

_____

_____

_____

_____

_____

_____

_____

_____

In your eyes, what is the most difficult part of your job as a financial crime fighter?
How do you handle it?

_____

_____

_____

_____

_____

_____

_____

_____

_____

_____

_____

_____

_____

Do you have a unique or interesting financial crime-fighting story that you can share?

_____

_____

_____

_____

_____

_____

_____

_____

_____

_____

_____

_____

_____

_____

_____

What do you think is the most effective strategy to fighting financial crime?

_____

_____

_____

_____

_____

_____

_____

_____

_____

_____

_____

_____

_____

_____

Do you believe there is more that we can do to fight financial crime? If so, what more?

_____

_____

_____

_____

_____

_____

_____

_____

_____

_____

_____

_____

_____

_____

What would you change about financial crime risk and compliance programs?

_____

_____

_____

_____

_____

_____

_____

_____

_____

_____

_____

_____

_____

_____

_____

What is the role of technology in your current job?
Do you think it will be more critical with the threat of COVID-19?

_____

_____

_____

_____

_____

_____

_____

_____

_____

_____

_____

_____

_____

_____

If financial crime fighters want to stay relevant in this coming age of A.I. and machine learning technologies, what do you think are the most important steps for them to take?

_____

_____

_____

_____

_____

_____

_____

_____

_____

_____

_____

_____

_____

Knowing what you now know, what are some mistakes you've made that you want other financial crime fighters to learn from or avoid?

_____

_____

_____

_____

_____

_____

_____

_____

_____

_____

_____

_____

_____

_____

Is there any one mistake you find financial crime fighters making over and over in their careers?

_____

_____

_____

_____

_____

_____

_____

_____

_____

_____

_____

_____

_____

What failures have you learned from the most that have contributed to your career success?

_____

_____

_____

_____

_____

_____

_____

_____

_____

_____

_____

_____

_____

_____

When you hear the term 'career success', what/who comes to mind? What are your top 3 tips for career success?

_____

_____

_____

_____

_____

_____

_____

_____

_____

_____

_____

_____

_____

_____

_____

Was there ever a time when you wished you took a different career path? Why did you decide to stay in/ return to financial crime?

_____

_____

_____

_____

_____

_____

_____

_____

_____

_____

_____

_____

_____

_____

How do you feel about mentoring? Do you believe that it can help in developing a financial crime fighter's career? Are there any mentoring stories that you can share?

What is your typical daily schedule? Do you have any hints for managing work-related stress? How do you stay productive?

_____

_____

_____

_____

_____

_____

_____

_____

_____

_____

_____

_____

_____

_____

It can be challenging to find time for yourself in any career.
Do you have any helpful tips on how to do this successfully?

_____

_____

_____

_____

_____

_____

_____

_____

_____

_____

_____

_____

_____

If you could give advice to your younger self just entering our profession, what would it be?

_____

_____

_____

_____

_____

_____

_____

_____

_____

_____

_____

_____

If you had a chance to get a message out to all Financial Crime Fighters in the world, what would you write?

_____

_____

_____

_____

_____

_____

_____

_____

_____

_____

_____

_____

_____

_____

CLOSING THOUGHTS

Congratulations on completing the book. Here are five recommendations on what to do next.

1. If you have not already done so, please write your responses to the 18 questions, and if you send them to me at book@thefinancial-crimes.com, parts of your answers might get featured should there be a volume 2 to this book.

2. The lessons and insights you found here were hard-earned by some of the best in the world in our profession. It is possible that you have not absorbed everything by reading it once. Start the book again. Make it a habit to read at least 5 minutes a day, reflect on what you read for another 5 minutes, and then act. Doing this might change your life and career in ways you never dreamed possible.

3. I would love to have your help spreading the message. If you liked the book, please consider spreading the word to your friends and colleagues so that more people can learn the wisdom offered here. The practical learnings shared in this book are essential but not taught in any seminar or training course.

4. If you got immense value from this book, consider gifting a copy to others who you think might benefit as well. You will make a difference to that person's life and be remembered as the person who introduced the book to them. You will also be making a difference in the fight against modern slavery as all profits from the sale of this book will forever be donated to charity.

5. Most important of all, ACT. Do not let this book just sit in your Kindle library or on your shelf, collecting dust. Do something. Try anything. You do not get changes in your life or career by just reading. You get changes by acting.

I cannot wait to see and hear about your progress. You are going to change the world, I know it.

On behalf of my co-authors, John Cusack, Marta Lia Requeijo, Nicholas (Nick) Turner, Mel Georgie B. Racela, Anthony Nappi, Jerome Michailidis, Lucy Masters, Jason Holt, Rod Francis, Scott Burton, Armina Antoniou, Carlos Garcia Pavia, Paul (Paddy) O'Hara, Will Brown, Dr William Scott Grob, Jessica Hodson, Guillermo (Memo) Horta, Marlene Meli, Stevenson (Steve) Munro, Maggie Qiu, Jaikumar (Jai) Ramaswamy, Patricia (Trish) Sullivan, Martin James Wallis, John Fogarty, Matt Friedman, Yvette Cheak, Eric Favila, Anthony Quinn, Abtar Randhawa, and Deborah Young, I would like to close by saying we are honoured to play a tiny part in your journey to a successful and fulfilling life and career.

Tadeo (Jun) Claravall
Financial Crime Fighter

ABOUT THE PUBLISHER

We are dedicated to helping financial crime fighters gain higher-level skills, clarity, and confidence to fight financial crime.

Your job is difficult. You deal with high stakes situations every day, and there are severe consequences for your organisation and your career if you make the wrong decision.

We equip you with knowledge and tools to make better business and risk decisions, so you have peace of mind that you are doing the right things, reducing your risk, and keeping your organisation out of trouble.

Go to www.thefinancialcrimes.com to receive more information about our workshop, scorecard, and podcast.

Printed in Great Britain
by Amazon